Cambridge Elements

Elements in Chinese Economy and Governance
edited by
Luke Qi Zhang
Fudan University
Mingxing Liu
Peking University
Daniel Mattingly
Yale University

RETHINKING POLITICAL MERITOCRACY

An Attention-Based Approach

Xiao Ma
Peking University

CAMBRIDGE
UNIVERSITY PRESS

CAMBRIDGE
UNIVERSITY PRESS

Shaftesbury Road, Cambridge CB2 8EA, United Kingdom

One Liberty Plaza, 20th Floor, New York, NY 10006, USA

477 Williamstown Road, Port Melbourne, VIC 3207, Australia

314–321, 3rd Floor, Plot 3, Splendor Forum, Jasola District Centre, New Delhi – 110025, India

Cambridge University Press is part of Cambridge University Press & Assessment, a department of the University of Cambridge.

We share the University's mission to contribute to society through the pursuit of education, learning and research at the highest international levels of excellence.

www.cambridge.org
Information on this title: www.cambridge.org/9781009502672

DOI: 10.1017/9781009502702

First published 2026

A catalogue record for this publication is available from the British Library

A Cataloging-in-Publication data record for this Element is available from the Library of Congress

ISBN 978-1-009-50267-2 Hardback
ISBN 978-1-009-50271-9 Paperback
ISSN 2976-5625 (online)
ISSN 2976-5617 (print)

Rethinking Political Meritocracy

An Attention-Based Approach

Elements in Chinese Economy and Governance

DOI: 10.1017/9781009502702
First published online: May 2026

Xiao Ma
Peking University

Author for correspondence: Xiao Ma, x.m@pku.edu.cn

Abstract: Political meritocracy, which selects and promotes officials based on their work performance, is an important explanation for China's rapid development. While prior studies focus on territorial leaders (*kuai*), less attention is given to functional department leaders (*tiao*), whose performance is harder to measure, attribute, or compare. This Element introduces an attention-based explanation, arguing that in China's complex bureaucratic system, marked by intricate divisions of labor and information asymmetry, capturing superiors' attention is critical for officials' career advancement. Through case studies and analyses of original biographical data on functional department leaders, this Element reveals: (1) Promotion likelihood correlates with officials' ability to gain superiors' attention; (2) not all attention-seeking behaviors align with governance goals, often fostering bureaucratic issues like formalism and over-implementation. This attention-based framework tries to reconcile debates on competence versus connections in Chinese political selection and explains both the bureaucratic system's successes and its governance challenges.

Keywords: meritocracy, attention, promotion, bureaucracy, China

ISBNs: 9781009502672 (HB), 9781009502719 (PB), 9781009502702 (OC)
ISSNs: 2976-5625 (online), 2976-5617 (print)

Contents

1 Introduction

The selection of high-quality officials has a profound impact on government performance (e.g., Evans & Rauch, 1999; Jones & Olken, 2005). China's remarkable achievements in economic and social development over the past half-century have been attributed by many scholars to its merit-based official selection system. Officials who excel in policy areas prioritized by their superiors are more likely to be promoted, and this selection mechanism in turn provides high-powered incentives for officials to achieve the goals set by their superiors (e.g., Bo, 1996; Whiting, 2001; Li & Zhou, 2005). Some scholars and China watchers argue that this merit-based political selection system (i.e., political meritocracy) constitutes a core feature of the "China model," distinct from Western-style electoral systems (e.g., Bell, 2015). This Element reviews classic empirical studies on political meritocracy and finds that the vast majority focus on the leaders of territorial party committees and governments at various levels (i.e., province, municipality, county, and township), with very few analyzing the heads of functional departments (e.g., transportation, health, education, and public security), which are also critical components of the regime. A key prerequisite for political meritocracy is that officials' performance can be measured, attributed, and compared – an assumption more readily met among heads of territorial administrations (Maskin, Qian, & Xu, 2000; Zhou, 2007). So, how can we explain the behavioral logic of functional department leaders, whose performance is more difficult to measure, attribute, and compare? In the past decade or so, the functional departments (the so-called *tiao*) have been endowed with increasingly significant powers and roles (Cao & Wang, 2020). Understanding the incentive structures that influence their behavior is also of great practical significance for comprehending Chinese politics.

To address the above question, this Element proposes an alternative explanation of political selection based on attention allocation: The key to an official's career advancement lies in their ability to capture the attention of superiors. Psychological research has found that human attention is limited, and individuals can only focus on and process a limited number of matters at any given time (e.g., Broadbent, 1958; Simon, 1971; Shiffrin, 1988). In an encompassing Leninist regime like China, the socioeconomic affairs managed by the government are extremely diverse, leading to complexity of bureaucratic divisions and hierarchies and asymmetry in governance-related information (Lu & Ma, 2020). The attention of superior leaders can hardly be evenly distributed across all matters handled by each department. At any given time, leaders' attention tends to focus on only a few select areas (Chen, 2021). For departments whose performance is not easily measurable, work performance is not an objective metric but a quality that can be packaged, interpreted, or even exaggerated, making the capture of superiors' attention particularly crucial. This Element argues that an official's ability to gain superior attention depends on a combination of factors, including the inherent characteristics of their department (e.g., whether its function aligns with superior's policy priority, whether it grants more access to superiors), the official's proactive efforts (e.g., creating exemplary cases from their work, leveraging media publicity), and the impact of exogenous events (e.g., changing public opinion). However, not all efforts by officials to gain the attention of superiors are conducive to governance objectives. This Element argues that some subordinates' strategic efforts to capture superior attention may lead to numerous bureaucratic pathologies, including the long-standing phenomena of formalism and bureaucratism in Chinese politics.

The empirical analysis of this Element is divided into two parts. First, we collected and analyzed the biographical information of 2,759 cadres who served as heads of provincial government functional departments between 2012 and 2022. After controlling for factors such as age, education, gender, ethnicity, work experience, and relationships with superiors, we found that their promotion probabilities were significantly and positively correlated with two variables measuring the allocation of superior attention. One is the frequency with which the work of the department is mentioned in the provincial government work report, and the other is the Baidu Index that measures the online search intensity for each department in its respective province. While the government work report serves as a direct measure of superior's attention allocation, the Baidu Index, reflecting real-time online public sentiment, provides an indirect measure. Furthermore, we tested the external validity of the study's core argument by analyzing the career trajectories of heads of bureaus within the Ministry of Foreign Affairs (MFA), confirming that bureau heads whose work involves greater access to superior leaders (and thereby their attention) are more likely to be promoted. Second, we developed a typology of grassroots officials' policy implementation behaviors based on two dimensions: the clarity of superior policy objectives and the incentive mechanisms employed. Through a content analysis of 939 typical cases of formalism and bureaucratism published by provincial Commissions for Discipline Inspection between 2020 and 2024, we explained how superiors' limited attention leads subordinates to strategically seek attention or evade accountability, resulting in bureaucratic pathologies such as non-implementation, over-implementation, and performative implementation.

This Element reexamines China's political selection through the lens of human attention (Simon, 1971; March & Olson, 1983). Classic theoretical work on organizations has systematically explored how information shapes organizational performance and members' behavior (e.g., March & Simon, 1958; Williamson, 1975; Jensen & Meckling, 1976; Milgrom & Roberts, 1988). Drawing on the Chinese context, this study analyzes the impact of superiors' attention allocation on officials' career advancement and governance behavior. The findings contribute to a deeper understanding of Chinese politics in two key ways. First, while most empirical research on political selection focuses on the heads of local governments,[1] the attention-based framework enables us to expand the scope of analysis to include heads of functional departments, which are also critical components of the regime. The data collected and analyzed on provincial government department heads provide firsthand evidence for systematically understanding the individual characteristics and career development patterns of this group. Second, the argument of this Element seeks to bridge the long-standing debate in the literature on Chinese political selection regarding the roles of competence and connections.[2] Most existing arguments view merit-based promotion as conflicting with patronage-based promotion. However, under the attention-based framework, the underlying logics of competence and connections are similar. Whether through outstanding performance in one's role or through close personal ties with superiors, both serve the same purpose: capturing the attention of higher-ups who control an official's career trajectory. In a vast bureaucratic system rife with information asymmetry, any means by which a subordinate can get recognized by superiors with limited attention become a significant advantage. This analytical framework also helps us understand why China's bureaucratic system achieves remarkable success in some areas while facing governance challenges in others.

This Element is organized as follows. Section 2 reviews the existing studies on political meritocracy, highlighting that the assumptions about the measurability, attributability, and comparability of performance have led most research to focus on territorial leaders, while the behavioral logic of leaders of equally important functional departments remains underexplored. Building on insights from various disciplines, this section proposes an alternative explanation based on attention. Section 3 first introduces the characteristics of provincial government functional department leaders using an originally collected dataset. Then, through analysis of this data and a case study of the MFA, this section demonstrates how the allocation of superior attention influences the promotion probabilities of department leaders. Section 4 first establishes a typology of officials' policy implementation behaviors based on the clarity of superiors' policy intentions and incentive mechanisms. Then, through analysis of typical formalism and bureaucratism cases published on provincial Commission for Discipline Inspection websites, the section illustrates how subordinates' efforts to gain superior recognition or evade accountability under limited superior attention led to various distortions in policy implementation. Section 5 concludes and discusses the findings.

---

[1] See Section 2.2 of this Element for a review.

[2] See Manion (2023) and Su & Tao (2024) for comprehensive reviews of the debate.

2 Political Meritocracy and an Attention-Based Alternative Approach

2.1 Defining Political Meritocracy

Political meritocracy refers to a system in which the allocation of political power is "in accordance with ability and virtue" (Bell, 2015, p. 6). The term meritocracy was coined by English sociologist Michael Young (1958) in his fiction *The Rise of the Meritocracy*, which described a future dystopian society where people's statuses are determined by intelligence and effort. The term has since then gained traction in fields such as education, economics, and political philosophy, being used to describe systems that reward individuals with talent, ability, effort, or a combination of any of those (e.g., Sandel, 2020).

In the context of China, political meritocracy refers specifically to the ways in which the ruling Communist Party of China (CPC) selects and promotes officials (Bell, 2015). Unlike in Western democracies, where there is a clear division between government bureaucrats and elected politicians, in China the boundary is blurred. The CPC appoints all party and government officials at different levels, even in some nominally social organizations such as hospitals, schools, and state-owned enterprises (Manion, 1985; Burns, 1989; Chan, 2004). A large body of theoretical and empirical studies have suggested that the party evaluates officials' performance on a regular basis and rewards and promotes officials that outperform their peers (e.g., Bo, 1996; Maskin, Qian, & Xu, 2000; Whiting, 2001, 2004; Edin, 2003; Li & Zhou, 2005). Such a system in turn generates high-powered incentives for officials at different levels to exert efforts in areas deemed important by their superiors, such as economic development, social stability, and environmental protection (e.g., Whiting, 2001; Lü & Landry, 2014; Zuo, 2015; He, Wang, & Zhang, 2020).

The political meritocracy this Element examines has the following scopes. First, this study focuses on the dynamics *after* an individual has entered the party state (e.g., performance evaluation, and promotion), although competitive recruitment of public officials is also an important feature of political meritocracy (e.g., Wang & Yang, 2025). Existing studies have shown that those who enter civil service through the highly competitive civil service exams differ significantly from the rest of the population in biographical characteristics, such as education, gender, and family background (e.g., Liu, 2019; Jiang, Shao, & Zhang, 2022). Second, while evaluation and performance-based promotion affect essentially all members of the party state, I focus on the leading officials (i.e., cadres) here.[3] This

[3] While ordinary officials in non-leading positions are also subject to performance evaluation, their career paths (and thereby incentives) differ significantly from those of the leading officials (Ang, 2016).

group includes leaders of territorial administrations (i.e., provinces, cities, counties, and townships), and those of functional departments (e.g., finance, transportation, social security, healthcare, and public security) at different levels of governments. These two types of institutions are traditionally known as "*kuai* (territorial administration)" and "*tiao* (functional departments)" in Chinese politics. Third, this study not only examines the institutions, both formal and informal, that manage personnel in China, more crucially, it also looks at how officials respond to these institutions and whether such responses contribute to the goals of the state.

The topic of political meritocracy has generated perhaps the most extensive scholarly debate in the field of Chinese politics. Some of the foundational work in the topic has been cited more than 2,000 times to date (e.g., Li & Zhou, 2005; Xu, 2011). Manion (2023) conducts a thorough review of this literature, and elucidates the main challenges to the political meritocracy thesis. First, some scholars argue that the promotion of officials is not determined by merit, but instead driven by officials' connection with their superiors. This line of argument can be traced back to the discussion of factional politics in China (Nathan, 1973; Nathan & Tsai, 1995; Shih, 2008; Francois, Trebbi, & Xiao, 2023). Instead of maximizing governance performance, the ruler seeks to maximize their chance of political survival by rewarding offices and other spoils to those who are loyal to them (e.g., Bueno de Mesquita et al., 2005; Hicken, 2011). A large number of empirical research indeed document a positive correlation between officials' connections with their superiors, mostly proxied by shared work experience, and their chances of promotion in China (e.g., Shih, Adolph, & Liu, 2012; Opper, Nee, & Brehm, 2015; Keller, 2016; Fisman et al., 2020; Su & Tao, 2024). The connection argument undercuts the very foundation of meritocracy and suggests patronage as an alternative logic in governing personnel selection (Scott, 1972), although there is also research suggesting that appointing trusted subordinates to important positions might mitigate principal-agent problem and enhance governance performance (Jiang, 2018). Some other scholars have also suggested that patronage and meritocracy are not necessarily contradictory and might complement one another (Jia, Kudamatsu, & Seim, 2015; Wang, Yao, & Zhang, 2022).

The second strand of criticism of political meritocracy mostly focuses on methodological issues. To begin with, the literature's overemphasis on the causal effect of a few key metrics (e.g., GDP) on promotion neglects more nuanced institutional practices in cadre appointment such as age limits and horizontal transfers (Manion, 2023). Officials at different levels face explicit age limits for promotion, and those who surpass the specified ages are no longer eligible for further promotion (Kou & Tsai, 2014). This means that not every official in the same jurisdiction is incentivized by performance evaluation. Furthermore, while most empirical analyses only code an outright upward move in bureaucratic hierarchy as promotion, many horizontal transfers (i.e., from a less important position to a more important position with equal rank) also constitute de facto promotion (Wong & Zeng, 2018). Neglecting these practices in statistical analyses might cast doubt on the robustness of their conclusions. As Manion (2023) puts it, "the age constraints introduce omitted variable bias, [and] the so-called 'lateral transfers' introduce measurement error (p. 45)." Scholars have also questioned whether GDP serves as an accurate measure for performance as officials can manipulate local economic data to enhance their chance of promotion (e.g., Wallace, 2016). In some occasions, officials might even bargain with their superiors to negotiate more favorable evaluation criteria, suggesting the possibility that performance might be endogenous to one's political connections (Leng & Zuo, 2022). In addition, some other studies have also shown that the selection and promotion logic of officials might differ depending on the rank, and performance-based promotion is mostly salient at the grassroots level (i.e., county) (e.g., Landry, Lü, & Duan, 2018; Wiebe, 2024).

2.2 The Hidden Assumption of Political Meritocracy

The notion of political meritocracy, which posits that officials are selected based on performance, rests on a critical assumption: that performance is a tangible entity that can be observed, measured, and compared across individuals. In practice, however, this assumption is challenging to fulfill. Public choice scholars have long highlighted the differences between political organizations (e.g., bureaucracies) and economic entities (e.g., firms), noting that the former are not subject to the same competitive pressures as the latter (Tullock, 1965; Niskanen, 1971). Unlike firm managers, whose performance is largely evident through market outcomes, bureaucratic leaders are far harder to evaluate objectively. The effects of government officials' decisions often take years to manifest, and linking specific governance outcomes to individual behaviors is also complex and uncertain.

To effectively horserace government officials against one another, their performance needs to be measurable and attributable to individuals who deserve the credit. Measurability means that no matter how complex the process of governance is, its outcomes should be observable and can be reduced to measures such as numbers. Attributability means that the evaluators can clearly identify the individuals responsible for the specific outcomes they observe. In constructing the theoretical model of the "promotion tournament," Zhou (2007) proposed several technical conditions that must be met, including (1) "the existence of an objectively measurable competition metric from the perspective of both the principal and the agent," and (2) "the 'competition performance' of the participating entities, i.e., government officials, is relatively separable and comparable" (p. 40). These two conditions correspond to measurability and attributability, respectively.

In most occasions, measurability is a prerequisite for attributability. If one cannot observe or measure certain outcomes, then it might also be difficult to attribute the outcomes to certain individuals. The publicity department of local party committee, for example, is responsible for building spiritual civilization (*jingshen wenming*) in a locality. This objective is much more difficult to quantify compared with economic growth or investment attraction, and it is also affected by numerous factors often beyond the control of a local jurisdiction. Measurability however does not automatically entail attributability. It is possible that policy goals that are easy to measure are difficult to attribute. Take population policies, for example. It is not difficult to measure the outcomes of population policies – one only needs to look at the changes in demographic statistics. But since population growth requires concerted efforts and cooperation among numerous bureaucratic domains, such as healthcare, education, labor, and social welfare, it becomes very difficult, if not impossible, to attribute the growth (or the lack thereof) of population to any individual bureaucracy.

Additionally, the performance of different departments needs to be comparable, meaning their performance can be measured by the same metric. When a department's performance cannot be measured or attributed, comparison is clearly difficult; however, even if an individual department's performance can be clearly measured or attributed, it does not necessarily mean that comparisons between departments are feasible. For example, the performance of the Commerce Department is typically measured by the amount of investment attracted, while the Finance Department is evaluated based on the amount of tax revenue collected. Although both are quantifiable metrics, comparing them is akin to comparing apples and oranges.

Meeting the three conditions of measurability, attributability, and comparability is not easy, and often requires officials involved to take specific organizational forms. Economists have found that the multidivisional form (M-form) of firms, one that was organized into several equivalent entities each producing similar products, has higher profits than the unitary form (U-form) of firms, one that was organized into several functional departments coordinated by a superior to produce one product (Chandler, 1962; Williamson, 1975). M-form organizations perform better because they are much easier to measure, attribute, and compare the performance of subordinate units, as they are roughly equal in their endowments, and independently produce similar products. The subordinate units of U-form, in contrast, differ significantly in their functions and the output they produce. In one of the classical papers that apply this insight to understand the incentive structure facing subnational leaders, Qian and Xu (1993) argue that the Chinese government system differs importantly from the Soviet system, as the latter was organized as a U-form consisting of numerous specialized ministries (e.g., steel and cotton), whereas the Chinese system has resembled an M-form, with a large number of comparable, and self-sufficient subnational regions (e.g., provinces and cities). Subsequent empirical analyses of the framework indeed find that the M-form organization of the Chinese system provides better incentives and spurs yardstick competition among subnational leaders (Maskin, Qian, & Xu, 2000).

Building on these insights, Zhou (2014) conceptualizes China's intergovernmental relations as "administrative subcontracting," whereby higher-level authorities "subcontract" responsibilities for subordinate regions to local leaders. The center retains a few critical levers of power – such as control over personnel appointments, issuing general policy guidance, and the right to intervene – while delegating most policy decisions to local officials. The advantage of this arrangement is that the center need only evaluate a small set of governance outcomes (e.g., economic growth, revenue collection, social stability, and environmental protection) across regions to identify and reward competent subordinates. In turn, under this tournament-style selection system, local leaders are incentivized to compete to achieve the goals favored by their superiors. According to Zhou (2014), the incentive structure embedded in administrative subcontracting is most pronounced in territorial administrations (e.g., provinces, cities, and counties) and helps explain both the successes and the failures of China's governance. For instance, Zhou (2014, p. 29) notes that the central government subcontracts the task of training Olympic champions to provincial sports administrations, which helps explain why China tends to excel in individual sports (e.g., diving, shooting, table tennis, and weightlifting) rather than team sports (e.g., soccer, basketball, and volleyball). This is because performance in individual sports is much easier to measure and attribute than performance in team sports – which draw athletes from multiple provinces – thereby giving local governments stronger incentives to invest in individual disciplines.

It is therefore not surprising that most existing empirical studies on political meritocracy focus on the economic performance of territorial leaders (e.g., provinces, cities, and counties). Table 1 surveys articles published on the subject in some of the leading social science journals, and two conspicuous patterns emerge. First, an overwhelming majority of them focus on territorial leaders (e.g., provincial, municipal, and county party and government leaders). Second, almost all of them use economic indicators (e.g., GDP and revenue growth) of the territories as proxies for officials' performance. One notable exception is Lee

Table 1a Selected empirical studies on political meritocracy

Studies	Performance measures	Performance as[a]	Officials examined	Time period
Bo (1996)	Average GDP growth; net fiscal contribution; per capita income	X	Provincial party secretaries and governors	1949–94
Landry (2003)	Population; per capita GDP; share of service sector GDP; foreign direct investment	X	Municipal mayors	1990–2000
Li & Zhou (2005)	Annual GDP growth; average GDP growth during time in office	X	Provincial party secretaries and governors	1979–95
Shih, Adolph, & Liu (2012)	Relative GDP growth; relative fiscal revenue growth	X	Central Committee members and alternate members	1982–2007
Su et al. (2012)	Per capita GDP growth; differences in per capita GDP growth between incumbent and predecessor; differences in per capita GDP growth with neighboring provinces	X	Provincial party secretaries and governors	1979–2002
Zhang (2014)	GDP growth	X	Provincial party secretaries	1990–2007
Yao & Zhang (2015)	"Leader effects"[b]	X	Municipal party and government leaders	1994–2010

Table 1b (cont.)

Studies	Performance measures	Performance as[a]	Officials examined	Time period
Jia, Kudamatsu, & Seim (2015)	Annual real GDP growth	X	Provincial party secretaries and governors	1993–2009
Landry, Lü, & Duan (2018)	Relative fiscal revenue and GDP growth	X	Provincial, municipal, and county party and government leaders	1996–2007
Li, Liu, Weng, & Zhou (2019)	GDP growth as a share of provincial five-year plan growth target and of provincial government work report target	X	Municipal party secretaries and mayors	2003–14
Wang, Yao, & Zhang (2022)	"Leader effects" [c]	X	Municipal and provincial party and government leaders	1994–2017
Lei & Zhou (2022)	Obtaining subway projects approval	X	Municipal mayors	2003–16
Li & Manion (2023)	Relative fiscal revenue and GDP growth	X	Municipal party secretaries	2013–17
Lee & Schuler (2019)	Public profile in Baidu trend index	X	State council ministers	2005–16
Guo (2009)	Annual fiscal expenditure growth	Y	County party and government leaders	1998–2002
Kung & Chen (2011)	Grain procurement	Y	Provincial first party secretaries and governors	1956–66

Table 1c (cont.)

Studies	Performance measures	Performance as[a]	Officials examined	Time period
Wallace (2016)	Differences between reported GDP growth and electricity growth	Y	Provincial party secretaries and governors	2000–09
Li & Yu (2023)	Per capita fiscal revenue	Y	Municipal party secretaries	2003–07
Jia (2024)	Emission of pollutant	Y	Provincial governors	1993–2010
Xue & Zhang (2024)	Industry-use land sales	Y	Municipal party secretaries and mayors	2007–17

Notes:

[a] X denotes performance measures are used as explanatory variables, and Y denotes performance measures are used as outcome variables.

[b] In Yao & Zhang (2015), leader effects are calculated by estimating the leader fixed effects on economic growth for those leaders who have served in multiple localities, after accounting for factors such as city and year fixed effects.

[c] Similar to Yao and Zhang (2015), Wang, Yao, and Zhang (2022) estimate leader effects by following the strategy adopted in Yao & Zhang (2015).

and Schuler (2020), which studies the effect of political competence on ministers' career advancement. They argue that an official's political competence is best manifested through their ability to garner public attention, and they use Google Trends and Baidu Index data to measure the size of an official's public profile.

These empirical analyses however leave out many important questions unanswered. First, as explained earlier, economic growth of a region is a rare situation in which governance outcomes can be easily measured and linked to the presiding territorial leaders, but it only reflects one aspect of governance. For many other policy areas, the "merit" of officials in charge cannot be easily measured or compared. For example, healthcare, public safety, and cultural development are three policy domains no less important than economic development. The performance of the corresponding bureaucracies however is much more difficult to measure than economic growth, let alone comparing the three. In some occasions, the demonstration of bureaucratic "merit" even goes against the very purpose that an agency was founded. For example, the number of criminal cases solved is an important indicator of local public security agency's performance. Yet the occurrence of criminal cases per se suggests that local public security has room for improvement. Similar situations exist for a wide range of bureaucratic agencies, such as safety regulation, national security, and media censorship. These agencies share a dilemma: If they do their job really well, then there will be no job left for them to do. Over time, they will be neglected by their superiors, their budget and payrolls will be cut, and even their very existence will be questioned.

Second and relatedly, we know very little about the career dynamics and the underlying incentives other than those of the territorial leaders. As noted in Section 2.1, leaders of functional departments (*tiao*), who are in charge of specific policy domains and enjoy the same ranks as leaders of subordinate territorial administrations (*kuai*), consist of another important group of officials in the party state. They are larger in number (compared to *kuai* leaders),[4] and are also competitive candidates for higher-level positions. Table 2 shows that

[4] The number of functional department leaders varies based on localities and ranks. Take province, for example. A province's bureau-level functional department leaders typically consist of the following: about ten leaders of the departments (bureaus) in the provincial party committee (usually the executive deputy director of the department), about thirty-five to forty directors of provincial government bureaus (and commissions), about fifteen to twenty bureaus (and commissions) directors in the provincial people's congress, and about fifteen to twenty bureau (and commissions) directors in the provincial people's political consultative conference. In contrast, a province on average has about ten to eleven municipalities, which means there are about thirty to forty bureau-level territorial leaders (i.e., municipal party secretary, mayor, chairpersons of the municipal people's congress, and people's political consultative conference. In many occasions, the municipal party secretary concurrently chairs the municipal people's congress (Yang, 2024).

Table 2 Exit options of provincial bureau leaders (2012–22, $N = 2{,}676$)[a]

Status after[b]	Percentage
Promotion[c]	23.9%
Lateral move[d]	50%
Demotion[e]	5.6%
Corruption investigation[f]	4.5%
Retirement	11.3%
Resignation	0.2%
Others[g]	4.5%

Notes:

a. Data is compiled by the author. The unit of observation is leader of bureau in provincial government. If an individual was the head of two different bureaus in sequence, then it counts as two observations. Bureau leaders of provincial party committee, provincial people's congress, and provincial people's political consultative conference are not counted.

b. This column lists the conditions in which a bureau leader left their office.

c. Promotion refers to situations in which a bureau head is either (1) promoted to a deputy provincial (ministerial) position (e.g., member of the provincial party standing committee, deputy governor, deputy chairperson of the provincial people's congress standing committee, or the provincial people's political consultative conference, party secretary, or mayor of sub-provincial city) or (2) appointed as a party secretary of regular prefecture. Prefectural party secretary is often considered as the most consequential bureau level (*zhengtingji*) position in a province (Jiang, 2018, p. 989).

d. Lateral move refers to situations in which a bureau head is transferred to head another bureau, appointed as the head of a provincial state-owned enterprise or social institution (*shiye danwei*) with equivalent rank, or appointed as the mayor of a regular prefecture.

e. Demotion refers to a situation in which a bureau head is appointed to a lower-ranked (e.g., deputy bureau level or section level) position. This is usually the result of receiving disciplinary punishment.

f. This category means the officials are arrested for corruption investigation and are completely removed from their offices.

g. This category includes (1) death while in office, and (2) still in the same office at the time of data collection (July 2024).

among those who served as heads of provincial government bureaus between 2012 and 2022, nearly one-fourth of them were promoted to more important positions. We however know very little about what helps them realize their career aspirations and what determines why some of them get promoted while others don't.

The paucity of empirical evidence in these dimensions is certainly not an accident. Researchers who intend to examine the career incentives of functional departmental leaders perhaps face the same dilemma as those who manage U-form organizations: It is empirically difficult to measure and compare the performance of drastically different departments. Therefore it is not a coincidence that most government statistics include disaggregated data of subordinate regions, but very few of them include statistics by subordinate departments.[5] Functional department leaders, who are experienced bureaucrats, should also be keenly aware of this issue facing the researchers and their superiors. How would they strategize their behaviors to circumvent this structural limitation and maximize their chances of advancement, and what consequences these actions have on policymaking and implementation?

2.3 An Attention-Based Explanation

This Element attempts to construct an attention-based explanation to address the aforementioned questions. The core argument of this Element is that officials need to gain the attention of their superiors to obtain various resources, including career advancement. However, whether they can secure the attention of superior leaders is not necessarily determined by whether the specific work outcomes they are responsible for are easily measurable, or by whether they work in territorial governments or functional departments. At the same time, the behaviors of subordinate officials in gaining superior attention do not always necessarily contribute to the goals of national governance. I will first introduce this argument by systematically reviewing existing research on attention from various disciplines.

The systematic scientific inquiry on human attention began in the field of psychology. Attention is defined as "all those aspects of human cognition that the subject can control, and to all aspects of human cognition having to do with limited resources and capacity, and methods of dealing with such constraints" (Shiffrin, 1988, p. 799). It is characterized by its limited capacity to process information, and the fact that individuals can consciously control the allocation of their attention (Styles, 2006, p. 1). Early research on attention conceptualizes the human perceptual system as a "filter": While people constantly receive numerous information, the nervous system allows only some classes of stimuli to pass, rather than all (Broadbent, 1958, pp. 41–42). Subsequent research has focused on the timing of the information-filtering process (Deutsch & Deutsch,

[5] Some functional lines (such as transportation and healthcare) publish statistical yearbooks that include numbers of subordinate agencies in different provinces. But not all functional lines publish statistical yearbooks, nor can their numbers be compared meaningfully across different domains.

1963), and the influences of alertness, selectivity, and processing capacity on attention (Posner & Boies, 1971). Treisman (1969) summarizes four mechanisms of selective attention: selection of output, selection of input (or sets of sensory data for analysis), selection of analyzers, and selection of tests and targets. Overall, these studies have all highlighted the limited capacity of human attention.

Building on the insights from psychology, social science scholars in economics and management studies have treated human attention as a scarce resource. Herbert Simon, for example, noted that when faced with an overwhelming volume of information, an individual's attention becomes a scarce resource, prompting consumers to avoid squandering their focus aimlessly. Concurrently, due to people's limited capacity to process information, businesses must invest substantial resources to capture consumer attention, thereby securing effective market dominance – a phenomenon dubbed the "attention economy" (Simon, 1971, p. 53). In the internet-driven era of an "information explosion," attention allocation is further characterized as "playing a hegemonic role" (Citton, 2017, p. 10). Within management studies, attention theory has been employed to elucidate corporate strategic decision-making. Ocasio (1997), for example, argues that organizational behavior arises from how a firm channels and distributes decision-makers' attention, which in turn shapes the company's prioritization of time and effort in tackling problems, opportunities, and threats. Subsequent research highlights that the modes of information communication also influence the process of directing attention allocation (Ocasio, Laamanen, & Vaara, 2018).

Scholars in political science and public administration have likewise identified the crucial role played by attention in shaping various policy outcomes. March and Olson (1983), for example, recognize that leadership attention is a scarce resource, and that securing the attention of relevant political actors becomes a prerequisite for those who seek to drive policy changes. Jones and Baumgartner (2005) point out that "attention is a severe constraining factor in politics – a bottleneck through which all matters must squeeze" (p. 250). The process by which politicians' attention is allocated to some problems rather than others is known as agenda setting. Actors who are better at supplying information to the decision-makers, such as through hiring professional lobbyists to persuade politicians, are more likely to get their preferred policy treatment (e.g., Austen-Smith, 1993; Goldstein & You, 2017; Payson, 2020). Jones and Baumgartner (2005) however argue that the allocation of politicians' attention (and thereby their policy choices) might not be perfectly proportional to the amount of information they receive. The human nature of selective attention, combined with sporadic exogenous shocks (such as breaking news), produces a "disproportionate information-processing model" (Jones & Baumgartner, 2005) that explains why policy changes often follow the pattern of a "punctuated equilibrium" (Baumgartner & Jones, 1993; Baumgartner et al., 2009) rather than that of incrementalism.

While the prevailing theoretical analysis on the political implications of attention is situated in the study of American politics, scholars of Chinese politics have also paid a substantial amount of attention to the subject. Chen (2021) uses the written directives (*pishi*) of Chinese national leaders to study the determinants of allocation of leadership attention. He argues that the allocation of leadership attention is affected by objective factors such as leaders' political status and health conditions, as well as subjective factors such as the perceived importance and urgency of the issues and leaders' policy preferences. The allocation of national leaders' attention in turn has important consequences. Using data from 1949 to 1976, Chen, Christensen, and Ma (2019) find that central agencies that received more written directives from Chairman Mao, a proxy they use for political salience, were less likely to get terminated, and they also find that peripheral agencies (i.e., smaller, lower-ranked agencies with noncore functions) benefited more from leaders' attention. In another related research, Chen, Christensen, and Ma (2024) show that leadership attention, also proxied by the number of written directives from Chairman Mao received by each ministry, was significantly correlated with ministerial leaders' longevity in offices during China's politically tumultuous decades before the reform and opening-up, and that the effect of leadership attention was more pronounced than that of one's shared historical connections with Mao.

Superiors' attention not only plays an important role in high-level elite politics, it also figures prominently in grassroots governance in China.[6] Chen and Gu (2022) contend that Chinese local cadres face a variety of tasks assigned by their superiors, and the key to a successful career is to wisely allocate their efforts to areas that can attract the attention of their superiors and in turn gain the superiors' recognition. This incentive structure explains why even in developing the local economy local leaders tend to prioritize investments that are more visible to their superiors, such as building roads and bridges, instead of investing in education or maintaining the sewerage system (e.g., Wu & Zhou, 2018; Leng, 2025). In recent years, the central government's priority has gradually shifted from economic development to social management, rendering it more difficult to numerically measure the performance of local cadres. Recognizing this shift, some local leaders strategically cultivate closer bonds between their jurisdictions (*kuai*) and functional departments (*tiao*) for public service and social management at higher or equal level. Such tiao-kuai pairs enable localities to experiment with various governance innovations and gain a better

[6] For a synthesis of the attention-allocation framework at the grassroots level, see Lian (2015).

visibility in the "impression-based evaluation" among issue areas deemed important by their superiors (Huang & Zhou, 2019).

Like in American politics, gaining the attention of superiors is often a prerequisite for localities to secure policy benefits in China. Despite being highly decentralized in social and economic governance (Xu, 2011), Chinese localities (i.e., provinces, cities, and counties) still benefit from various kinds of resources and regulatory power in the hands of central government, such as transfers, subsidies, designation of special policy zones, and approval of large investment projects. Localities seeking such policy benefits however need to outcompete their peers to make sure their requests will be heeded and agreed upon by various central agencies, but this process is often not easy (Ma, 2022). Localities come up with innovative strategies to achieve this goal. Ji and Ma (2025), for example, find that Chinese counties mobilize retired revolutionaries as lobbyists in their pursuit for railway investment projects, which require central government approval. Retired revolutionaries can circumvent various bureaucratic ranks and pass localities' demand directly to the national leader, who can in turn exert pressure on central bureaucracies to make decisions preferred by the localities. The revolutionaries' moral authority as the founders of the regime makes their requests difficult to ignore, and consequently counties that have retired revolutionaries lobby on their behalf enjoy a notable advantage in securing central investments. Ma and Ma (2024) show that the reason why many Chinese cities are enthusiastic in hosting costly international mega events with limited prospects for returns (e.g., sports and cultural events and leadership summits) is that such events attract the attention of national leaders, who see such events as good opportunities to project national strength and often attend in person. As a result, localities that succeeded in bidding for such events can extract substantial policy benefits (e.g., infrastructure investments) from the central bureaucracies, often beyond the direct needs of the mega events.

Drawing from these insights, this Element argues that attention plays a central role in structuring the career incentives (and thereby the behaviors) of functional department leaders. This Element shares a common ground with the political meritocracy thesis by assuming that public officials, regardless if they are in functional departments or territorial administrations, are career maximizers who seek promotion, pay raise, and (or) enlarged budgets. But officials achieve their goals primarily through capturing the attention of their superiors. Superiors hold power and resources that affect the careers of their subordinates. Unlike subordinates, who oversee specific policy domains (i.e., departments), superiors are responsible for a much wider range of issues, and the amount of attention they can spend on each issue is very limited. Having the attention of superiors is the prerequisite for a bureaucratic domain (and its leaders) to obtain resources (and seek career advancement). Demonstrating merit (i.e., doing actually well in one's job) is only one way among many to capture the attention of superiors. For numerous policy domains in which bureaucratic merit cannot be easily measured or observed, officials might engage in activities that deviate from their designated responsibilities to gain the attention of their superiors.

The central role of superiors' attention in shaping officials' career incentives is most evident in the promotion process. Under the 2019 Regulations on the Selection and Appointment of Party and Government Leading Officials,[7] appointing a cadre entails multiple formal stages – democratic recommendation (*minzhu tuijian*), assessment (*kaocha*), and collective deliberation and decision (*taolun jueding*) – with the final decision made by the party committee at the next higher level that oversees the post.[8] Before these stages begin, however, there is a preliminary "motion" (*dongyi*) phase: the party's organization department submits to the higher-level party secretary a report indicating the need to promote a cadre;[9] only with the secretary's approval may the department proceed with the subsequent steps.[10] This pivotal step gives the leader of the higher-level party organization substantial influence over personnel appointments. When consulted on whether to initiate the selection process, a party secretary who already has a preferred candidate will often recommend that person to the head of the organization department; such informal recommendations can significantly shape the ensuing formal procedures, effectively setting the agenda.[11] The candidates a party secretary can put forward at this initial stage are typically lower-level officials they know personally or have heard about. Once the organization department launches the formal process, the result of each step must be reported to higher-level leaders, and cadres who are more familiar to those leaders are more likely to advance through the successive rounds of screening.

[7] The document was first issued in 1995 and subsequently revised in 2002, 2014, and 2019. According to Manion (2023, p. 9), it is the CPC's most important document governing the appointment of officials.

[8] See, Gov.cn, "Regulations on the Selection and Appointment of Party and Government Leading Officials" [in Chinese], www.gov.cn/zhengce/2019-03/17/content_5374532.htm, last accessed October 21, 2025.

[9] The specific timing for introducing the motion is described only vaguely in Article 11 of the Regulations as "based on work needs and the actual circumstances of leadership team development." In practice, such situations typically include the incumbent reaching the mandatory retirement age, being transferred to another post, or coming under investigation, among others.

[10] See Article 13 of the Regulations.

[11] Interview with a provincial party organization department official in central China, March 18, 2025.

A common view holds that higher-level leaders often place their trusted confidants in important posts in advance to gain experience and build credentials for future promotion. In such cases, whether an official attracts the leader's attention is endogenous to their relationship: Leaders assign confidants to departments that oversee the policy areas they prioritize, giving these subordinates more opportunity for direct interaction. This phenomenon does exist in practice. Under the CPC's "cadre training" (*ganbu peiyang*) system, cadres who are trusted by their superiors are rotated through important – and thus more visible – departments and are more likely to be promoted later (e.g., Pang, Keng, & Zhong, 2018). Consequently, what truly propels their advancement is their close personal tie to the superior, rather than the superior's attention to the department per se.[12]

That said, the existence of this mechanism does not falsify the attention mechanism emphasized in this study; the two can coexist and be complementary. The number of trusted confidants available to any superior is far *smaller* than the number of appointments they must make. The elaborative hierarchy of the party state (i.e., nomenklatura) encompasses numerous positions that span across the party, the government, various social organizations, and state-owned enterprises (Manion, 1985; Burns, 1989; Chan, 2004). According to a provincial party organization department official in central China, the number of provincially managed cadres, whose appointments require the approval of the provincial party standing committee, is close to 2,700 in that province alone.[13] Existing studies show that the network size of most people's acquaintances is no greater than 150 (e.g., Hill & Dunbar, 2003). It is simply beyond the capacity of any individuals to recognize and remember the names and faces of this many people, let alone to have the detailed knowledge of the quality of these individuals. Lu and Ma (2020) use two anecdotes to illustrate how this information problem arises from the complexity of the party state's bureaucracy.

> Mao Zedong sacked Li Dongye, an official in the CCP General Office in 1958, but Li assumed a leadership position in Liaoning province soon thereafter without Mao's knowledge (Qi, 2016, p. 164). The decentralization of power and proliferation of agencies in the post-Mao era make the problem

[12] In the empirical analysis in the next section, we account for this alternative explanation by controlling for the connections between officials and their superiors.

[13] This group includes leaders of provincial party, government, people's congress, and people's political consultative conference departments (bureaus, commissions) and their deputies, leadership of municipalities, leadership of provincial level social organizations (such as universities and hospitals) and provincial state-owned enterprises, and some county party secretaries and executives. The number of centrally managed cadres, whose appointments require the approval of party's central leadership, is between 3,000 and 4,000. Interview with a provincial party organization department official in central China, March 18, 2025.

> worse. Yang Weize, then party secretary of Wuxi – a major industrial and commercial hub – had been unknown to Zhou Yongkang (then domestic security chief and a Wuxi native), until Zhou's brother introduced Yang to Zhou. (p. 67)

This kind of information asymmetry should not be a surprise to any seasoned regime insiders. A crucial step to have one's superior to entrust them with important positions or responsibilities is to make sure that one's name would come up first when their superiors deliberate on the issue. In a randomized field experiment, de Janvry et al. (2023) divided 3,785 Chinese township officials who were fresh out of colleges into two groups. These young officials were under a two-year contract, and upon completion their evaluation on the job would determine whether they could get a highly competitive, permanent contract. These officials each had two superiors and only one of their assessments (i.e., the evaluator) would determine the fate of the officials. The researchers revealed the identity of the evaluators in one group and concealed it in another. They find that in the revealed group, the officials diverted considerably more efforts to please the evaluators, including spending more efforts in tasks assigned by the evaluator and placing a higher value in maintaining personal relationships with the evaluators (what the authors term "influence activities"). In the masked group, in contrast, the officials spent equal efforts on tasks assigned by both superiors. The researchers also find that in the revealed group, the evaluating superior, whose identity was revealed to the officials, gave significantly more positive assessment than her nonevaluating counterpart, suggesting the impact of subordinates' influence activities on superiors' judgement.

Whether an official can gain the attention of superiors depends on numerous complex factors. First, the characteristics of the official's department play a significant role. When a department's work area aligns with the current policy priorities of senior leaders, its head naturally attracts more attention. In some cases, although a department's work may not directly relate to the leaders' policy concerns, it may still offer frequent opportunities to interact with leaders (e.g., departments handling logistics for leaders), making it easier for their heads to gain attention. Beyond departmental characteristics, the proactive efforts of individual officials also play a crucial role. In Chinese officialdom, a common phenomenon is that after a leadership transition, subordinate officials often engage in extensive discussions about the characteristics of the new leader, particularly in comparison to their predecessor. These discussions cover differences in the new leader's work priorities, styles, habits, personal interests, and interpersonal relationships. Such discussions can be seen as rational subordinates attempting to recalibrate the "parameters" of the new superior's preferences in order to more effectively gain their attention and recognition through various strategies.

Milgrom and Roberts (1988) pointed out that in organizations, the attempts by subordinates to influence the behavior of their superiors can be divided into two types. Some can be productive, meaning these behaviors contribute to achieving the organization's goals, while others may be nonproductive, such as when some subordinates attempt to bribe their superiors to gain favor. In China, the behaviors of subordinates in government departments to gain the attention of their superiors can also generally be categorized into these two types, though their specific manifestations are more diverse. First, when the outcomes of a superior's work tasks are relatively easy to measure (e.g., economic growth, fiscal revenue collection, or investment attraction), the simplest way for subordinates to gain the superior's attention is to strive to stand out among their peers in their work. When a previously unknown subordinate official consistently performs exceptionally well in policy areas that the superior cares about, they naturally attract the superior's attention. This mechanism aligns with the logic of the classic promotion tournament theory (Li & Zhou, 2005).

Second, when the outcomes of a superior's work tasks are not easily measurable or comparable, subordinates can still employ various methods to visibly demonstrate that their efforts align with their superiors' priority. One approach is to significantly increase work input. Classical studies have pointed out that when work outcomes are difficult to measure, organizational leaders tend to adopt input-based evaluations (e.g., Kerr, 1975; Jensen & Meckling, 1976; Ouchi, 1979; Wilson, 1989). Taking students as an example, a teacher can measure their learning effectiveness either using exam scores (output) or indicators such as attendance rates (input). For Chinese officials, the ways to demonstrate work input are also diverse. One method is to directly signal effort in a highly visible manner, such as frequently holding meetings to study the superior's directives or innovating local work methods to make them exemplary. Other methods of showcasing input are less visible, such as reporting work to superiors through internal references (*neican*) or directly seeking opportunities to meet with them to report progress.[14]

The media plays a significant role in the process by which officials gain the attention of their superiors. Although in China the government exerts strong control over the media, there are numerous market-oriented media outlets, such as commercial newspapers and social media platforms. Compared to official media, these outlets have greater freedom in reporting and, driven by profit motives, tend to cover content that interests readers (Stockmann, 2013).

[14] For a detailed study of the internal reference institutions, see Tsai (2015).

Officials with distinctive personal styles, outstanding political achievements, or adeptness at engaging with the media often receive more coverage. Existing research has shown that in Leninist states like China and Vietnam, there are "star officials" who garner significant media attention, similar to those in Western electoral systems (e.g., Gueorguiev & Schuler, 2016; Lu & Ma, 2020; Lee & Schuler, 2020). Commercial and social media can not only build large profiles for individual officials but also promote their work content, increasing media exposure for their fields of work and achievements. For example, after 2004, under the tenure of the then Railway Minister Liu Zhijun, China's high-speed rail achieved leapfrog development.[15] While the media gave Liu Zhijun significant personal exposure, it also greatly increased external attention to the development of Chinese railways (Ma, 2022, pp. 95–96). It is worth noting that while "good publicity" (i.e., coverage tied to achievements) certainly helps officials, neutral or even negative publicity (e.g., crises) sometimes can likewise put them front and center and capture the attention of superiors.[16] In many cases, the officials are not at fault; the incident simply brings an otherwise marginal jurisdiction to the attention of higher authorities. Additionally, officials can also leverage state media platforms under their direct control to enhance the visibility of their work achievements (e.g., Pan, 2019).

Last but not the least, personal connections also play an indispensable role in the process of gaining the attention of superiors. These personal connections are largely based on existing social ties, such as being from the same birthplace, classmates, or colleagues (e.g., Shih, Adolph, & Liu, 2012). This probabilistic measure of connections has been criticized for potential measurement errors, while other scholars have adopted a stricter standard – whether an individual was promoted during a superior's tenure – to measure the relationship between superiors and subordinates (e.g., Keller, 2016; Jiang, 2018). Of course, a significant number of connections are established through unobservable informal activities, with bribery being the most typical example.[17] For instance, as demonstrated in the investigation of the factional group led by former Deputy Minister of Public Security Sun Lijun, many members of his group established connections with Sun by directly bribing him.[18] Regarding the role of personal

[15] Liu, therefore, was also dubbed "Leapfrog Liu" by China's railway enthusiast (Ma, 2022, p. 95).

[16] For example, Sun Zexian, the then head of the Food Safety Department at the State Food and Drug Administration, came under intense media scrutiny during the 2008 milk scandal. In 2009, he received a temporary disciplinary measure; in 2012, he was promoted to deputy director of the State Food and Drug Administration.

[17] Zhu (2026), for example, finds that bribery constitutes a third pathway to political office, alongside performance and patronage.

[18] See Caixin.com, "Accepting bribes worth 440 million and offering bribes of nearly 100 million, 'Little Seafood' Wang Like was sentenced to death with a reprieve and lifelong imprisonment" [in Chinese], https://china.caixin.com/m/2022-09-22/101943400.html?refurl=https%3A%2F%

connections in gaining superior's attention, existing studies have proposed different mechanisms. Jia, Kudamatsu, and Seim (2015) find that personal relationships facilitate communication between superiors and subordinates, enabling superiors to receive stronger signals about subordinates' performance. As mentioned in Section 2.2, in many cases, a subordinate's performance is not self-evident, particularly in those less-measurable areas. Jiang (2018), on the other hand, argues that connections address the classic credible commitment problem in patron–client relationships,[19] fostering smoother cooperation between superiors and subordinates and making superiors more willing to trust and fully delegate authority.

The aforementioned approaches of gaining attention are not mutually exclusive. For example, officials who consistently outcompete their peers in completing tasks assigned by their superiors may also simultaneously receive significant media attention. Those who gain the attention of superiors by demonstrating input might also leverage media coverage to build momentum. Additionally, existing studies suggest that officials with better connections with their superiors are more willing to experiment with reform pilots (Jiang & Zeng, 2020) or have greater incentives to invest effort in completing tasks assigned by superiors (Jiang, 2018). Furthermore, it is also difficult to distinguish whether a particular approach is productive (i.e., contributing to organizational goals) or nonproductive. Even in the first category of behavior – gaining attention by diligently completing tasks assigned by superiors – there exists the possibility that subordinates selectively focus on a few highly visible goals, thereby distorting the true intentions of their superiors (Kerr, 1975; Holmström & Milgrom, 1991). In summary, it is difficult to measure an individual's ability to influence a superior's attention through a single dimension. As mentioned at the beginning of this section, the allocation of attention itself is a complex psychological process, and the process by which other actors generate influence over attention allocation is likewise complex. In the next two sections, we will demonstrate the impact of superior attention on officials' behavior.

3 Attention and Promotion

This section tests one of the core hypotheses proposed earlier, namely, that an official's career advancement is influenced by their ability to effectively capture the attention of superiors. The section first introduces an original database of heads of functional departments across China's thirty-one provincial governments from

2Fmappv5.caixin.com%2Fm_topic_detail%2F1688.html%3Fcxapp_topic%3D1688, last accessed April 3, 2025.

[19] For discussions on the credible commitment problem in patron–client relationship, see, for example, Hicken (2011) and Robinson & Verdier (2013).

2012 to 2022. Through descriptive statistics and comparisons with local territorial administration leaders (i.e., municipal party secretaries and mayors), it reveals the characteristics of this significant yet understudied group of officials. The second part of the section constructs two indicators of a department's ability to gain superior attention – based on the relevance between the core functions of provincial administrative departments and their respective provincial government work reports, as well as the search intensity of departments on the Baidu Index – and finds that both indicators have a significant and positive correlation with the chance of promotion of department heads. Finally, through a case study comparing the career paths of heads of internal departments in the Chinese MFA who were promoted to MFA leadership, the section further shows that the ease of gaining access to superior leaders has a significant impact on officials' advancement.

3.1 Introducing the Provincial Functional Department Heads Dataset (PFDHD)

To analyze the effect of superior attention on subordinate career advancement, we collected an original biographical dataset on 2,759 provincial functional department heads between 2012 and 2022.[20] These leaders headed twenty-nine government departments (e.g., reform and development, education, science and technology, industry and information technology, civil affairs, and finance) across thirty-one provincial units on Chinese mainland.[21] Table 3 presents a list of departments included in our dataset and their English abbreviations. To compile the data, we first obtain the names of department heads using provincial yearbooks and internet searches,[22] and then we construct the data using information from both published official resumés and Baidu encyclopedia

[20] In most occasions, the department heads also concurrently serve as the secretaries of the communist party committees in their departments. When a department leader is not a communist party member or in ethnic minority regions, in addition to the department leader there is often a separate individual serving as communist party secretary of the department, resulting in "dual leadership" in these occasions. Our dataset includes information on both individuals if the two positions (department head and party secretary) were held by two different individuals. Additionally, in provincial government departments, there are some non-leadership positions at the department level, such as inspectors (*xunshiyuan*), who hold the same administrative rank as department heads. Our data does not include these cadres.

[21] We limit the provincial functional departments to those with ministerial counterparts under the State Council, China's central government. We do not examine departments of provincial party committees, provincial people's congresses and provincial people's political consultative conferences. Provincial units include provinces, ethnic autonomous regions, and centrally administered cities (Hong Kong, Macau, and Taiwan not included).

[22] For those places without provincial yearbooks, we search for specific provincial department positions (e.g., director of Zhejiang provincial finance department) and limit the search results in specific time period (e.g., 2016) to obtain the list of names of department heads over the years.

Table 3 List of provincial departments in PFDHD (2012–22)

Chinese names	English names	Abbreviations
政府办公厅	General Office	GO
发展和改革委员会	Development and Reform Commission	DRC
教育厅（局）	Department of Education	DOE
科学技术厅（局）	Department of Science and Technology	DST
工业和信息化厅（局）	Department of Industry and Information Technology	DIIT
民族（宗教）事务委员会	Ethnic and Religious Affairs Commission	ERAC
公安厅（局）	Department of Public Security	DPS
民政厅（局）	Department of Civil Affairs	DCA
司法厅（局）	Department of Justice	DOJ
财政厅（局）	Department of Finance	DOF
人力资源和社会保障厅（局）	Department of Human Resources and Social Security	DHRSS
自然资源厅（局）	Department of Natural Resources	DNR
生态环境厅	Department of Ecology and Environment	DEE[a]
住房和城乡建设厅（局）	Department of Housing and Urban-Rural Development	DHURD
交通运输厅（局）	Department of Transport	DOT
水利厅（局）	Department of Water Resources	DWR
农业农村厅（局）	Department of Agriculture and Rural Affairs	DARA
商务厅（局）	Department of Commerce	DOC
文化和旅游厅（局）	Department of Culture and Tourism	DCT
卫生健康委员会	Health Commission	HC

Table 3 (cont.)

Chinese names	English names	Abbreviations
退役军人事务厅（局）	Department of Veterans Affairs	DVA[b]
应急管理厅（局）	Department of Emergency Management	DEM[c]
审计厅（局）	Audit Office	AO
外事办公室	Foreign Affairs Office	FAO
国有资产监督管理委员会	State-Owned Assets Supervision and Administration Commission	SASAC
林业厅	Department of Forestry	DOF (Forestry)[d]
监察厅	Department of Supervision	DOS[e]
城市管理委员会	Municipal Commission of Urban Management	MCUM[f]
市场监督管理厅（局）	Administration for Market Regulation	AMR[g]

Note:

a. Before 2018, DEE was known as Department of Environmental Protection (环保厅（局）).

b. DVA was established in 2018.

c. DEM was established in 2018.

d. DOF (Forestry) was abolished in 2018.

e. DOS was abolished in 2018.

f. MCUM operates in three centrally administered cities (Beijing, Tianjin, and Chongqing).

g. AMR operates in Beijing, Tianjin, Shanghai, Jilin, and Ningxia.

entries. Two teams of research assistants independently collected the data and cross-checked with one another afterward to ensure data reliability. The data include basic biographical information of departmental heads (e.g., age, gender, education, and party seniority), and more detailed information on their career trajectories (e.g., previous work experiences and job status after serving as department leaders).

Among the 2,759 officials, 2,095 (75.9%) served as heads of one department, 576 (20.9%) served as heads of two departments, 84 (3.1%) served as heads of three departments, and only one served in four departments. That individual is Hu Kaijiang in Xinjiang Uygur Autonomous Region, who served as the chairman of region's Economic and Information Technology Commission between 2013 and 2018, director of the region's Industry and Information Technology Department between 2018 and 2019, director of the General Office of the autonomous region government between 2019 and 2022, and as the party secretary and deputy director of the region's State-Owned Assets Supervision and Administration Commission between 2022 and 2023.

The descriptive statistics in Table 4 present a social portrait of those individuals who served as provincial functional department heads between 2012 and 2022. This group is predominantly composed of Han Chinese (87.5%) males (92%), with the majority serving in their home province (61.6%). Before becoming department heads, most of them had experience in various sectors,

Table 4 Descriptive statistics of provincial functional department heads

Variables	Obs.	Mean	Std. dev.	Min	Max
Biographical Information[a]					
Gender (female = 1)	2,742	0.080	0.271	0	1
Han ethnicity (yes = 1)	2,666	0.875	0.331	0	1
Age at appointment	2,660	52.623	3.498	34	60
Native of this province (yes = 1)	2,531	0.616	0.486	0	1
Overseas experience (yes = 1)	2,390	0.139	0.346	0	1
Professional title (yes = 1)	2,502	0.352	0.478	0	1
Initial Education					
High school or below	2,221	0.128	0.335	0	1
Vocational/associate degree	2,221	0.166	0.372	0	1
Bachelor's degree	2,221	0.527	0.499	0	1
Master's degree	2,221	0.127	0.333	0	1
Doctoral degree	2,221	0.052	0.222	0	1
On-the-Job Education[b]					
No on-the-job education (yes = 1)	2,515	0.238	0.426	0	1
Bachelor's degree	2,515	0.074	0.262	0	1
Master's degree	2,515	0.436	0.496	0	1
MBA degree	2,515	0.072	0.259	0	1

Table 4 (cont.)

Variables	Obs.	Mean	Std. dev.	Min	Max
Doctoral degree	2,515	0.18	0.384	0	1
On-the-job degree from party school	1,703	0.388	0.487	0	1
Previous Work Experience[c]					
Sent-down youth (*zhiqing*) experience	2,461	0.104	0.305	0	1
Private enterprise	2,451	0.015	0.12	0	1
SOEs	2,478	0.251	0.434	0	1
Public institutions	2,479	0.487	0.5	0	1
Communist Youth League	2,445	0.225	0.418	0	1
Party departments	2,518	0.468	0.499	0	1
Local governments	2,564	0.787	0.409	0	1
Central government	2,511	0.117	0.322	0	1
Experience as secretary	2,491	0.328	0.47	0	1
Previous position as regional party/government leader	2,499	0.369	0.483	0	1
Entire career in this department	2,560	0.163	0.369	0	1
Previous and current jobs in the same system	2,685	0.355	0.479	0	1
Tenure as Department Leader[d]					
Tenure length (years)	2,759	3.904	2.426	0.17	14.58
Party seniority at appointment (years)	2,139	28.547	5.111	6	41
Concurrent position as provincial leader	2,652	0.121	0.326	0	1
Previous job in this province	2,677	0.954	0.209	0	1
After job in this province	2,191	0.95	0.218	0	1
Status After[e]					
Promotion	2,676	0.238	0.426	0	1
Lateral move	2,676	0.500	0.500	0	1
Demotion	2,676	0.056	0.231	0	1
Corruption investigation	2,676	0.045	0.207	0	1
Retirement	2,676	0.113	0.316	0	1
Resignation	2,676	0.002	0.043	0	1
Death	2,676	0.002	0.047	0	1
Still in the same position[f]	2,676	0.043	0.204	0	1

Table 4 (cont.)

Variables	Obs.	Mean	Std. dev.	Min	Max
Promotion Statistics[g]					
Promotion rate by province (%)	31	24.382	8.986	8.75	52.632
Promotion rate by department (%)	29	21.554	12.455	0	53.659

Notes:

a. Overseas experience refers to time spent outside mainland China for education and work purposes. Professional title refers to professional qualifications such as medical doctor, engineers, architect, and professor.

b. On-the-job education (*zaizhi jiaoyu*) refers to part-time, degree education received after one began full-time work.

c. Previous experience refers to any positions held by the officials before serving as department leaders. Public institutions include state-run schools, hospitals, think tanks, research institutes, museums, and so on. Party departments include party's general office, publicity, organization, united work front, law and politics, and discipline and inspection departments at different levels. Local governments include any positions in township, county, and municipal governments (or their affiliated institutions). Experience as secretary refers to assistant positions in support of leaders at a higher level. Previous position as regional party-government leader refers to top executive positions in township, county, and municipal governments or party committees. Entire career in this department refers to the situation in which the officials were employed in the same department throughout their careers. Previous and current jobs in the same system refers to the situation in which a department leader's immediate prior appointment is also in the same department (or affiliated institutions).

d. Concurrent position as provincial leader refers to the situation in which a department leader simultaneously holds the position as a member of provincial party standing committee, deputy provincial governor, deputy chairperson of the provincial people's congress, or deputy chairperson of the provincial people's political consultative conference.

e. This section reports the career status after an official served as a department leader. For definitions of each variable, see notes in Table 2. *Still in office* refers to the situation in which the official stays in the same position at the end of observational period (December 2022) at the time of data collection (July 2024).

f. This indicates that the official still served the same position at the end of 2022 when we collected the data (July 2024).

g. Promotion rate by province is calculated as the percentage of officials who received promotion after serving as department leaders in one province during the observational period (2012–22). Promotion rate by department is calculated as the percentage of officials in different provinces who received promotion after serving as leaders of a particular department during the observational period.

including local government (78.7%), party departments (46.8%), public institutions (48.7%), and state-owned enterprises (25.1%). About 35.5% of these department heads held their previous position within the same department (mostly as deputy leaders), while 16.3% spent their entire careers within the same specialized system. At the time of their appointment as department heads, they had an average of over 28 years of membership in the CPC, with an average age of 52.6 years and an average tenure in the position of 3.9 years. For officials at the departmental level, the official retirement age is sixty, and the party's organization department typically does not consider cadres over the age of fifty-eight for further promotion. Despite lacking an age advantage, nearly a quarter of these department heads (23.8%) were promoted further after completing their tenure, becoming provincial leaders or party secretaries of prefecture-level cities. Half of them (50%) were laterally transferred after their tenure to serve as heads of other departments or mayors of prefecture-level cities.

These department heads are a group of well-educated professionals. Among their initial academic credentials, 70.6% hold a bachelor's degree or higher (master's or doctorate).[23] Additionally, 76.2% of the department heads pursued on-the-job education (*zaizhi jiaoyu*) after starting work, with 68.8% of them earning a master's or doctoral degree while working. The proportion of department heads with state-issued professional titles (e.g., medical doctor, professor, or engineer) reaches 35.2%, and 13.9% have long-term overseas study or work experience.

It should be pointed out that these department heads, based on their rank (*zhengtingji*), belong to the category of provincially managed cadres (*shengguan ganbu*). Their files are managed by the provincial party committee's organization department, and decisions regarding their appointment and removal are made by the standing committee of the provincial party committee. If they are further promoted to deputy provincial or ministerial-level cadres, their appointment and removal decisions are made by the party's central leadership. However, if they continue to serve in the same province after promotion, the central organization department will also seek opinions from the main leaders of the provincial party committee and government. Two statistical figures indicate that the career mobility of department heads is significantly influenced by the leadership of their province. First, 95.4% of these department heads held other positions within the same province before assuming their current roles. Second, after completing their current tenure, 95% of them moved on to other positions within the same province (Table 4).

[23] Initial academic credentials refer to one's full-time college or postgraduate education.

Nationwide, only 5% of department heads are involved in interprovincial appointments, which may be facilitated through central authorities.

Although department heads are at the same administrative level as municipal party secretaries and mayors, there are significant differences in the individual characteristics of these two groups. Tables 5 and 6 compare the cadres who served as municipal party secretaries and mayors with department heads between 2012 and 2020. It shows that cadres serving as leaders of prefecture-level cities are generally younger than department heads, with mayors having a more pronounced age advantage (2.9 years). The educational attainment of department heads is significantly higher than that of cadres in prefecture-level cities. Among municipal party secretaries and mayors, nearly 30% of cadres have a first degree that is a vocational or associate degree, while this proportion is only 16.6% among department heads. At the same time, the proportion of department heads with master's degrees exceeds that of municipal party

Table 5 Comparing municipal party secretaries and provincial department heads

Variables	MPS average	PDH average	Diff.
Age at appointment	51.825	52.48	−0.655***
Gender (Female = 1)	0.053	0.081	−0.028***
Han ethnicity	0.908	0.876	0.032***
Initial Education			
Vocational/Associate degree	0.297	0.166	0.132***
Bachelor's degree	0.661	0.523	0.139***
Master's degree	0.041	0.127	−0.086***
Doctoral degree	0.001	0.051	−0.050***
Professional title	0.269	0.358	−0.090***
Overseas experience	0.106	0.141	−0.035***
Central government work experience	0.11	0.118	−0.007
Years of tenure	3.525	4.139	−0.614***
Native of this province	0.654	0.615	0.039**

Notes:

a. MPS = Municipal party secretaries; PDH = Provincial department heads

b. The data on the MPS is from 2012 to 2020, and we extract the PDH data from the same period as a comparison group. Therefore, the average statistics for PDH in this table are slightly different from those in Table 4.

c. *** $p<0.01$, ** $p<0.05$, * $p<0.1$.

Table 6 Comparing municipal mayors and provincial department heads

Variables	MM average	PDH average	Diff.
Age at appointment	49.568	52.48	−2.912***
Gender (Female = 1)	0.064	0.081	−0.017*
Han ethnicity	0.833	0.876	−0.043***
Initial Education			
Vocational/Associate degree	0.279	0.166	0.113***
Bachelor's degree	0.692	0.523	0.169***
Master's degree	0.024	0.127	−0.103***
Doctoral degree	0.005	0.051	−0.046***
Professional title	0.272	0.358	−0.086***
Overseas experience	0.107	0.141	−0.034***
Central government work experience	0.094	0.118	−0.023**
Years of tenure	3.442	4.139	−0.698***
Native of this province	0.716	0.615	0.101***

Notes:

a. MM = Municipal mayors; PDH = Provincial department heads.

b. The data on the MM is from 2012–2020, and we extract the PDH from the same period as a comparison group. Therefore, the average statistics for PDH in this table are slightly different from those in Table 4.

c. *** $p < 0.01$, ** $p < 0.05$, * $p < 0.1$.

secretaries and mayors by about 9–10%, and the proportion with doctoral degrees is nearly 5% higher. The percentages of those with professional titles and overseas experience are also noticeably higher than among municipal party secretaries and mayors. Furthermore, the average tenure of department heads is approximately 0.8 years longer than that of municipal party secretaries and mayors. Given that the average tenure of municipal party secretaries and mayors is only 3.3 years, this difference (nearly 25%) is also statistically significant. The above comparison highlights the differences between department heads, who tend to be specialists, and territorial leaders, who are more likely to be generalists: department heads have received a better education, often possess specialized knowledge in their fields, and have more extensive work experience within their systems.

We consider "promotion" to encompass two scenarios when coding the biographical information of department heads. The first, straightforward scenario is when a department head is promoted to a deputy provincial-level position (such as a member of the provincial party standing committee or a deputy governor). The second scenario is when they are appointed as the party secretary of a prefecture-level city (i.e., municipality). In terms of administrative rank, although a department head is on the same level as a municipal party secretary, we believe the latter is a significantly more important position. Within a province, the number of prefecture-level cities is far fewer than the number of government departments, making the top leadership position scarcer.[24] In terms of responsibilities, a municipal party secretary, as the top official, oversees population, affairs, and fiscal resources that far exceed those of a single provincial department at the same administrative level. It can be argued that among all full-department-level (*zhengtingji*) positions in a province, the party secretary of a prefecture-level city holds the greatest actual power and serves as a critical stepping stone to higher positions. For most officials who eventually reach the upper echelons of the CPC (i.e., political bureau and its standing committee), the majority have experience as the party secretary of a prefecture-level city (Jiang, 2018, p. 989).

For two positions at the same administrative level, existing research has adopted a sequential approach to determine their relative importance, by comparing the significance of the roles held by officials before or after assuming these positions (e.g., Jia & Xu, 2018). We have not collected the complete resumes of all prefecture-level city leaders nationwide, but we have analyzed the situation in Zhejiang Province as a case study. Taking the cadres who served as municipal party secretaries in Zhejiang Province between 2012 and 2022 as an example, out of forty-four individuals, twenty-seven (61.4%) were promoted to deputy provincial-level positions following their tenure as party secretaries.[25] In contrast, during the same period, among the forty-four individuals who served as municipal mayors in the same province, none were promoted to deputy provincial-level positions after they finished their tenure as mayors. Instead, twenty-six (59.1%) were later appointed as municipal party secretaries, and fifteen (34.1%) were transferred to department head positions or other full-department-level roles (such as in provincial party committee departments, provincial public institutions, or state-owned enterprises). This stark contrast demonstrates that the political status of a municipal party secretary far exceeds that of a mayor. A similar disparity in status exists between municipal party secretaries and department heads. In our data, even when including transfers to municipal party secretary positions, only 23.8% of department heads achieved promotions, a figure significantly lower than the explicit promotion rate

[24] There are 333 prefecture-level cities (or prefecture-level administrative units) in mainland China. On average, each of the twenty-eight provinces (and ethnic autonomous regions) has 11.9 prefecture-level cities.

[25] We excluded those who served leadership positions in deputy provincial cities (i.e., Hangzhou, Ningbo).

for municipal party secretaries mentioned above (61.4%). In summary, in our coding of resumes, we classify a department head's appointment to a municipal party secretary position as a promotion, while an appointment to a municipal mayor position is coded as a lateral move.[26]

Based on the aforementioned coding principles, we can compare the career development of department heads serving in different departments and regions. Figures 1 and 2 illustrate the promotion patterns of department heads by department and province, respectively. Among the various departments, heads of the Development and Reform Commission, Public Security Department, General Office of the Provincial Government, and Finance Department have a significantly higher probability of promotion compared to other department leaders. Notably, more than half of the heads who served as directors of the Provincial Development and Reform Commission, a powerful economic regulatory agency, received further promotions. Additionally, departments such as Transportation, Industry and Information Technology, Human Resources and

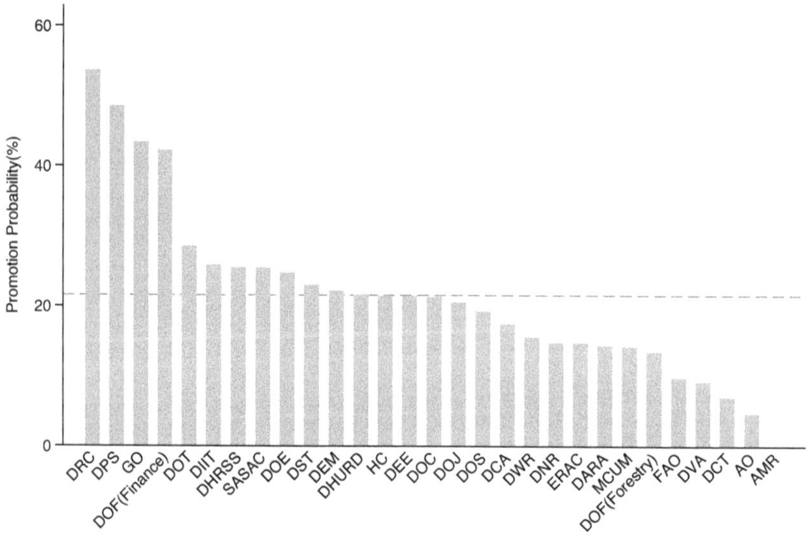

Figure 1 Promotion probability by department.

Note: The dashed line represents the average probability of promotion for all departments.

[26] We recognize the fact that there are many other lateral transfers that can be considered as implicit promotions (i.e., from a less important position to a more important position with equal rank). Unlike the situation of being appointed as a municipal party secretary, many of these implicit promotions are more idiosyncratic and harder to observe or measure systematically. We therefore do not further distinguish implicit promotions among lateral transfers.

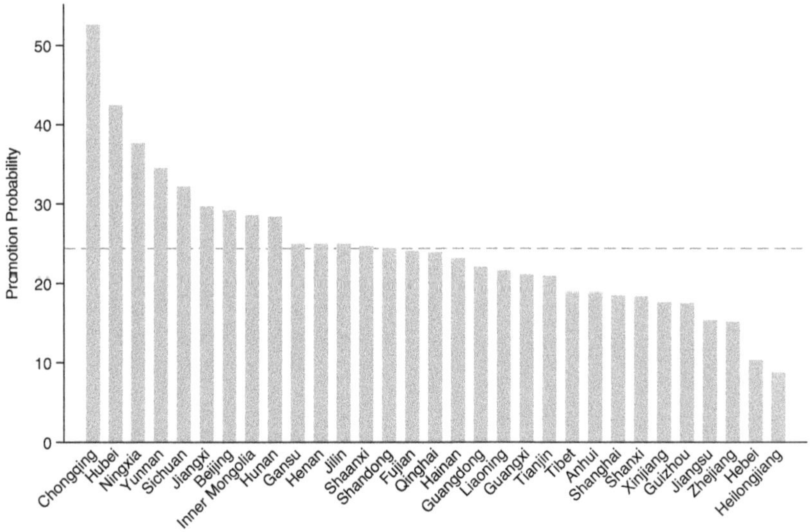

Figure 2 Promotion probability by province.

Note: The dashed line represents the average probability of promotion for all provinces.

Social Security, State-Owned Assets Supervision and Administration, and Education also exceed the average promotion rate. Departments with the least chances of promotion include Administration for Market Regulation, Audit Office, Culture and Tourism, Veterans Affairs, and Foreign Affairs Office. At the regional level, more than half of the department heads in Chongqing eventually secured promotions. Other provinces with higher promotion probabilities for department heads include Hubei, Ningxia, Yunnan, and Sichuan. Figure 3 further displays the average tenure of department heads across various sectors. In this dimension, the average tenure for most department heads ranges between three and four years, with only the General Office of the Provincial Government, Emergency Management Department, and Administration for Market Regulation having an average tenure shorter than three years.

3.2 Measuring Attention Allocation

The core argument of this study is that whether a department leader can achieve career advancement critically depends on their ability to effectively capture the attention of superiors. Ideally, measuring whether an individual's attention has been effectively captured would involve methods such as surveys or laboratory experiments. However, in this study, whether the department heads can achieve further promotion is determined by the provincial party leaders or the party's central leadership. Conducting longitudinal surveys among political elites at

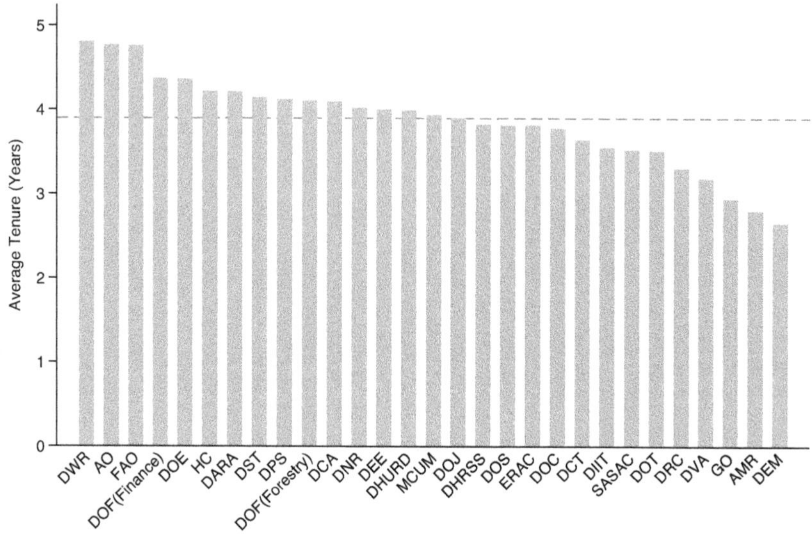

Figure 3 Average tenure (years) by department.

Note: The dashed line represents the average tenure (years) for all departments.

this level is clearly impractical.[27] This study instead employs indirect methods to measure this variable.

The first measure we use is the relevance of each government department's work content to the provincial government work report of that year, which proxies the degree to which a department's responsibilities align with provincial leaders' policy priorities. The government work report is presented by the provincial governor at the provincial people's congress meeting at the beginning of each year and is reviewed and approved by the congress. It generally consists of two parts: a summary of the government's work over the past year and the deployment and arrangement of the main tasks for the current year. These two parts provide detailed reports across different work areas, such as economic development, social affairs, culture, environmental protection, rule of law, and public safety. The coverage of these different areas often varies significantly in length based on their perceived importance. For example, in the 2024 Zhejiang Province government work report, when outlining the work plan for the new year, five sections were dedicated to economic development, while cultural development, environmental protection, and rule of law were each covered in only one section.[28]

[27] Some studies have conducted surveys with lower-ranked officials at the grassroots, for example, see Ma (2019).

[28] See Wang Hao, 2024 Zhejiang Provincial Government Work Report [in Chinese], www.zj.xinhuanet.com/20240129/369a0b5643e74342bc584affed26dcb9/c.html, last accessed April 22, 2025.

The drafting of the government work report involves a lengthy process. The leading agency (usually the policy research department of the provincial government), based on understanding the policy intentions of the provincial party and government leaders, collects opinions from various departments to form a draft. The draft undergoes review and revision by the provincial party committee's standing committee and further requires extensive consultation with various parties, including lower-level administrations (i.e., municipalities), leaders of democratic parties, scholars, entrepreneurs, and others. After the governor presents the report to the provincial people's congress deputies, the deputies can propose opinions to revise the report, though most revisions are minor and detail-oriented.[29]

Compared to our second measure (the Baidu Index score), the government work report more directly reflects the policy priority (and thereby attention allocation) of provincial leaders. During the drafting stage of the government work report, the provincial party secretary influences the report's content through written instructions and convening provincial party standing committee meetings to review and revise the report, while the governor personally serves as the chair of the drafting team. Areas where the main provincial party and government leaders invest significant effort typically receive more coverage than other areas. There is some correlation between the attention allocation of provincial leaders in the government work report and the issues of daily concern to the public (which we use as our second measure), but there are also significant differences. The former reflects the systematic considerations of provincial leaders for local development, while the latter is often influenced by short-term public opinion events. Departments aiming to increase their budgets or expand their influence will also attempt to lobby provincial leaders during the drafting process to gain more coverage for their work in this important document.[30]

To analyze the relevance of various departments to their corresponding province's government work report, we employ word embedding models to examine a dataset of the digitized provincial government work reports from 2012 to 2022. Word embedding algorithms generate a high-dimensional vector space by processing large amounts of digitized text, with each word represented by a vector in that space (Mikolov, Yih, & Zweig, 2013; Pennington, Socher, &

[29] In 2013, the Chinese Central Government published the detailed process through which its government work report was formulated. The drafting of the provincial work report generally follows the same procedures. See Gov.cn. The drafting process and the main content of government work report [in Chinese], www.gov.cn/test/2013-03/07/content_2347856.htm, last accessed April 22, 2025.

[30] Similarly, Ma (2022) found that, during the formulation of provincial five-year plans, prefecture-level cities with stronger bargaining power can secure greater coverage for their regions in the provincial five-year plan.

Manning, 2014). In this space, words with more similar contexts (i.e., content before and after the word) are closer together, while those with less similarity are farther apart. Word embedding models have been widely applied in social science research to analyze relationships between concepts and large text corpora (e.g., Kozlowski, Taddy, & Evans, 2019; Rodriguez & Spirling, 2022). In this study, we used key work-related terms from the names of provincial-level departments (e.g., "education" for the Education Department) as core "concepts" to be identified. Using word embedding models, we first extracted keywords from government work reports that are closely related to these concepts, and then calculated the number of concept-related keywords for each department in each year's government work report, with a higher number indicating greater relevance.

Taking the Education Department as an example, our coding procedure is as follows. First, we used the jiebaR package in R to perform Chinese word segmentation on government work report texts from 2012 to 2022. We also applied stop-word filtering and manually annotated fixed collocation phrases to optimize segmentation quality. Building on this, we trained a GloVe model using the text2vec package to learn distributed semantic vectors for words in their contexts, ensuring that words with similar meanings are closer in the vector space. Next, using "education" as the core concept, we retrieved the 200 most frequent words semantically similar to "education" in the vector space to construct an initial semantic expansion word list. This list included numerous education-related policy terms, such as "school," "preschool education," "higher education," and "compulsory education." Subsequently, we manually reviewed and refined the list, removing words with high ambiguity, or irrelevance to the concept, resulting in a final keyword dictionary. Finally, we employed a dictionary-based exact matching method to measure the association between the text and the concept. Specifically, this method counts the number of keywords in each document that exactly match the terms in the "education" keyword dictionary, with each keyword counted only once per document, regardless of multiple occurrences.

Some departments' Chinese names contain multiple keywords (e.g., Human Resources and Social Security, Ethnic and Religious Affairs),[31] while others have keywords that do not accurately reflect their core functions (e.g., General Office, Reform and Development). To avoid measurement errors, we excluded these departments from our sample, retaining twelve departments whose Chinese keywords accurately reflect their core functions (namely, Science and

[31] Arbitrarily summing or averaging the counts of related keywords for different concepts can lead to significant measurement errors.

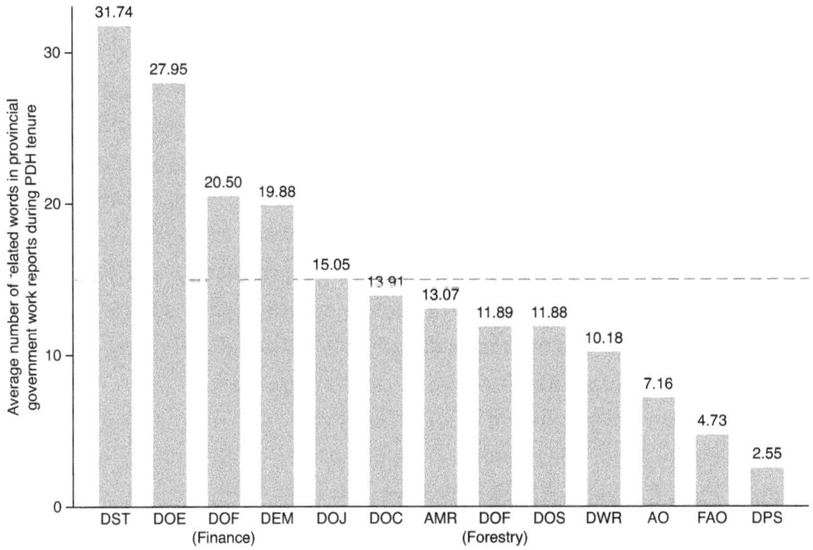

Figure 4 Comparing the relevance index of different departments to provincial government work reports.

Note: The dashed line represents the average number of the twelve departments.

Technology, Education, Finance, Emergency Management, Justice, Commerce, Market Regulation, Forestry, Supervision, Water Resources, Audit, Foreign Affairs, and Public Security).[32] Among these twelve departments, eight overlapped with the sample using the Baidu Index measure discussed in the next paragraph. In robustness checks, we also separately tested these eight departments for which data were available from both metrics. Figure 4 shows the average relevance index of the twelve departments across provinces to the provincial government work reports, calculated using the word embedding model.

The second measure is the average Baidu Index score of the functional department where a department head served during their tenure. Baidu is the largest search engine in China, with 700 million monthly active users.[33] The Baidu Index score reflects the scale of searches for a specific keyword by internet users, with the index rising when a keyword is frequently searched. For our study, one advantage of the Baidu Index is its ability to provide fine-grained data on the search intensity for a given keyword in a specific time period

[32] The Department of Emergency Management (DEM) was created in 2018, while the Departments of Forestry (DOF) and Supervision (DOS) were abolished in the same year. In our analysis, we use data between 2018 and 2022 for DEM and data between 2012 and 2018 for DOF and DOS.

[33] For data on the monthly active users, see 2024 Baidu Annual Trending Report [in Chinese], www.199it.com/archives/1734010.html, last accessed April 12, 2025.

(e.g., a particular year) and a specific region (e.g., a province). Similar to the construction of the relevance index, we used keywords corresponding to provincial department names (e.g., public security, science and technology, finance, and transportation) to construct a panel data of departmental search indices by province and year.[34] It should be noted that Baidu's province-specific index search only includes keywords for ten departments: education, finance, public security, science and technology, transportation, water resources, commerce, land resources, foreign affairs, and forestry.[35] Consequently, our subsequent data analysis is limited to these ten departments. Although this represents only a partial sample, these departments already cover multiple domains, including economy, sociocultural affairs, security, and foreign affairs.

We consider each department's Baidu Index score also to be an ideal, indirect measure for the attention it receives from higher-level authorities, based on two reasons. First, China has 1.108 billion internet users, with an internet penetration rate of 78.6%.[36] Senior officials at both the provincial level and the center, as a well-educated group, are themselves part of the internet user population and pay attention to various trending topics online. For example, Cai Qi, an incumbent member of Standing Committee of the Political Bureau of the CPC Central Committee and the first secretary of the CPC Secretariat, used to actively post on his microblog account and interact with his millions of followers before he was promoted to serve positions in Beijing.[37] Second, existing studies have found that the Chinese government exhibits a high degree of responsiveness (e.g., Lorentzen, 2014; Chen, Pan, & Xu, 2016; Truex, 2016; Distelhorst & Hou, 2017; Meng, Pan, & Yang, 2017; Jiang, Meng, & Zhang, 2019). Government officials use various channels to gather information on trending social issues and public concerns, making corresponding policy adjustments. This is considered one of the key mechanisms explaining the resilience of the Chinese system (Nathan, 2003). There is good reason to believe that when events related to a provincial department's work become a trending issue online, either due to

[34] There can be many keywords related to the work content of a department. To avoid bias caused by arbitrary selection, we only used keywords from the department's name for searches when constructing the index.

[35] The land resources and forestry departments were abolished or reorganized in 2018, we therefore only collect their data between 2012 and 2018. Data for public security is between 2014 and 2022 as data before 2014 was unavailable.

[36] See CCTV.com, China's internet user base reaches 1.108 billion, with an internet penetration rate rising to 78.6% [in Chinese], https://content-static.cctvnews.cctv.com/snow-book/index.html?item_id=14882213033316213332&t=1737091324176&toc_style_id=feeds_default&share_to=copy_url&track_id=526009ff-e049-48b8-9466-f4982e4b02c9, last accessed April 12, 2025.

[37] See, CCTV.com, Cai Qi named acting mayor of Beijing, used to be known by netizens for his microblogs [in Chinese], https://m.news.cctv.com/2016/10/30/ARTIvS95HH4pQutRa2VUafhi161030.shtml, last accessed April 21, 2025.

official's proactive efforts or by external forces, higher-level leaders will take notice of that department (and its leader) through various channels. Third, one might worry that the observed correlation between the relevance index and promotion is spurious: unobserved factors – such as patronage ties – could simultaneously raise the likelihood that an official's portfolio attracts leadership attention (e.g., more mentions in higher-level government work reports) and the official's chances of promotion.[38] By contrast, the Baidu Index captures topic-search intensity among millions of ordinary users and thus offers a plausibly exogenous proxy for the attention each department receives, less directly shaped by elite networks.[39]

Figure 5 shows the average scores across the country for the ten departments with available data on Baidu Index. The ranking among different departments aligns with intuition: departments closely related to the daily lives of ordinary people, such as public security, education, and finance, have higher search indices.

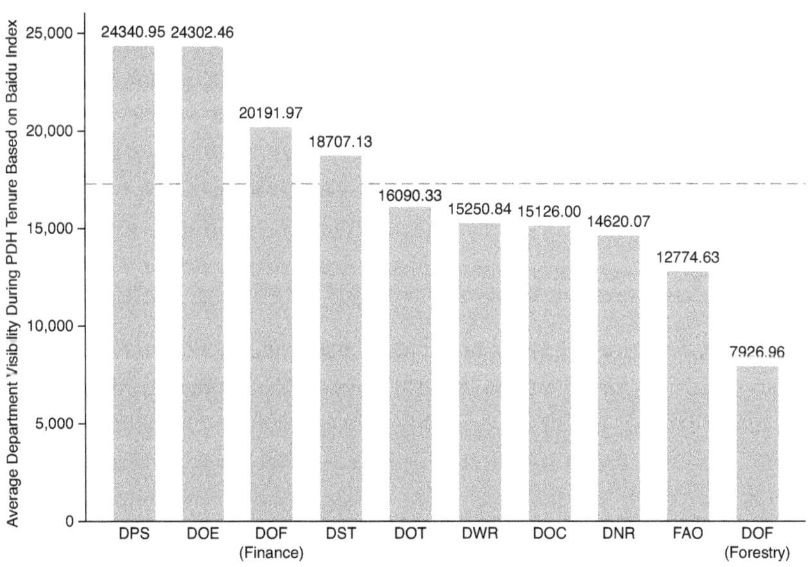

Figure 5 Comparing Baidu Index scores of different departments.

Note: The dashed line represents the average Baidu Index values of the ten departments.

[38] In the analysis for the relevance index score, we address this concern by controlling for the personal connections between the bureau heads and provincial leaders. Furthermore, in one of the robustness checks, we include provincial party secretary fixed effect to examine within-leader changes in the attention the departments get in the government work reports, and the results are consistent with those in the baseline model.

[39] We thank one anonymous reviewer for suggesting this point.

In contrast, departments less relevant to the lives of ordinary internet users, such as forestry, foreign affairs, and land resources, have lower search indices.

The Baidu Index ranking shows some similarity with that of the relevance index, such as the Science and Technology, Education, and Finance departments ranking high in both measures, while the Foreign Affairs and Water Resources departments ranking low in both. This correlation suggests that the policy attention of provincial party and government leaders is, to a large degree, driven by public concerns. A notable exception is the Public Security Department, which ranks first in the Baidu Index but last in relevance with government work reports. Although public security is a critical governance goal for local government, it is typically addressed sparingly in government work reports, as this work is led directly by the party's Political and Legal Affairs Commission. In our subsequent analysis, we conducted robustness checks using a sample that excluded the Public Security Department, and the results were largely consistent with those from the full sample analysis.[40]

Finally, it is important to note that both the relevance index and the Baidu Index score measure the attention a department receives, not the effort its leaders expend to attract that attention. As discussed in Section 2.3, superiors' attention is shaped by a combination of factors, including departmental characteristics, department leaders' proactive initiatives, and exogenous shocks. Because the level and form of department leaders' attention-seeking efforts are highly idiosyncratic and difficult to measure systematically, we focus on realized attention at the department level as our key explanatory variable.

3.3 Alternative Explanations and Estimation Method

Whether a department head is promoted depends not only on their ability to secure their superiors' attention but also on various other factors. We included a series of control variables in our analysis to rule out these competing explanations. First, age plays a significant role in cadre selection (e.g., Manion, 1993; Kou & Tsai, 2014; Yao & Zhang, 2015). Younger cadres, with greater potential for future promotions, may be more motivated to gain the attention of superiors. Higher-level authorities also consider the needs of cadre team-building

[40] Another reason for excluding the Public Security Department from the sample is that, in most provinces, the head of the Public Security Department is simultaneously appointed as a member of the provincial party standing committee or a deputy governor (Wang & Minzner, 2015). This concurrent appointment usually occurs shortly after the official assumes the role of department head and is primarily determined by the importance of the department, serving as a customary practice rather than a reward for the official's performance (Bulman & Jaros, 2019; Ma, 2022). Among all provincial government departments, only the head of the Public Security Department is consistently held by a deputy provincial-level leader, necessitating its exclusion from the sample to avoid potential bias.

(*ganbu tidui jianshe*) when selecting candidates of different age cohorts. The relationship between age and promotion probability thus may not be strictly linear, so we included a squared term for age in the regression to account for this possibility. Gender and ethnicity are also important considerations. Women and ethnic minorities may benefit from quotas in cadre selection for certain departments or levels (e.g., Jiang & Zhou, 2025), but they may face a glass ceiling at higher levels.[41] We included dummies to account for both identities. Educational background is another key factor, particularly for department heads leading highly specialized agencies (e.g., Zhou, 1995; Walder, Li, & Treiman, 2000; Zang, 2006). We included dummy variables in the regression for whether the department head's initial full-time education attainment is at the college level or above (postgraduate education), whether they received on-the-job education, and whether they hold professional titles. Existing research also suggests that cadres may exhibit different behavioral patterns at different stages of their tenure, particularly in how they construct their public image (Pan, 2019). Therefore, we controlled for the duration of the department head's tenure and its squared term.[42] Finally, as discussed in Section 2.3, informal networks also significantly influence cadre promotions (e.g., Shih, Adolph, & Liu, 2012). We controlled for this factor using two sets of variables. The first is a dummy variable for whether the department head was born in the province. Research has shown that birthplace ties are the most common vehicle for favor exchange in China (e.g., Fisman et al., 2018; Ji & Ma, 2025), giving locally born cadres a potential advantage in promotions. The second is the personal connections between the department head and the provincial party secretary or governor. Following Jiang's (2018) approach, we measured this relationship based on whether the department head was appointed to their current position during the tenure of a specific leader. Since the department head is a critical position, provincial leaders typically appoint only trusted cadres to such roles. As the tenures of the party secretary and governor do not always fully overlap, we separately measured the department head's relationship with each.

Following Landry, Lü, and Duan (2018), our unit of analysis is each department head.[43] Our outcome variable is a dummy indicating whether a department head was promoted after their tenure. For time-varying covariates such as age, tenure duration, and education level, we used data from the year the head's

[41] For example, in examining the determinants of ranks of party elites in the CPC's Central Committee, Shih, Adolph, and Liu (2012) find that ethnicity does not have a significant effect, whereas being women is negatively correlated with the rank in more recent party congresses, suggesting a potential penalizing effect of female gender in high-level elite politics.

[42] The rationale for including the squared term, as suggested by Landry, Lü, and Duan (2018), is that officials with an exceedingly long tenure might have a diminished chance for promotion.

[43] If an official served as director of two different departments, it is counted as two observations.

tenure ended. For political connection variables, we used measurements from the year the tenure ended in the baseline model, and also used the average connection status during the director's tenure as a robustness check.

Additionally, we controlled for province and year fixed effects in our analysis. Province fixed effects account for time-invariant factors, such as the number of prefecture-level cities under a province's jurisdiction, which may affect the likelihood of a provincial department head's promotion, or the long-standing political culture in a province.[44] Year fixed effects help control for the impact of specific years (e.g., large-scale cadre reshuffles before a party congress). We did not control for department fixed effects in the regression, based on two main considerations. First, as discussed in Section 2.3, a department's ability to effectively gain attention from higher authorities is inherently tied to its core responsibilities, which do not vary over time. It is possible that cadres who are more favored by higher-level leaders may be deliberately assigned to departments that more easily attract the attention of superiors while also being given more promotion opportunities. To rule out this possibility, we controlled for the personal connections between department heads and provincial leaders in our analysis. Second, including department fixed effects would imply horizontal competition and comparison among heads of the same department across different provinces, which does not conform to reality. A department head's primary competitors for promotion are other department-level cadres within the same province.

Since our dependent variable is a dummy measuring whether a department head is promoted, we used logistic regression in our baseline models. Considering regional differences across provinces, we also clustered standard errors for officials serving in the same province in some of our model specifications. To make the coefficient comparable, we also standardized the two measures of our key explanatory variable (i.e., relevance index and Baidu Index score) using z-score in our analyses.

3.4 Results and Robustness Checks

Tables 7 and 8 report the regression results using the relevance index of government work report and Baidu Index score as the core explanatory variables, respectively. In each table, Model 1 includes only the core independent variable, Model 2 adds other control variables, and Model 3 further controls for province and year fixed effects. Model 4 uses data excluding the Public Security

[44] We used the provincial fixed effects instead of the provincial leader (i.e., party secretary) fixed effect as we believe whether a provincial leader pays attention to a particular issue area could also be affected by innate personal characteristics, and including provincial leader fixed effect will absorb this important source of variations.

Table 7 Explaining promotion of provincial department heads using relevance index

	DV: Promotion					
	(1)	**(2)**	**(3)**	**(4)**	**(5)**	**(6)**
Variables	**Full**	**Full**	**Full**	**W/O DPS**	**Full**	**W/O DPS**
Relevance index	0.163**	0.340***	0.328***	0.770***	0.328**	0.770***
	(0.077)	(0.098)	(0.109)	(0.144)	(0.128)	(0.165)
Age		3.694***	4.582***	4.998***	4 582***	4.998***
		(0.893)	(1.045)	(1.202)	(1.664)	(1.859)
Gender (female = 1)		0.271	0.131	0.469	0.131	0.469
		(0.366)	(0.429)	(0.458)	(0.430)	(0.455)
Han ethnicity		0.491	0.854**	0.593	0.854*	0.593
		(0.352)	(0.416)	(0.443)	(0.500)	(0.531)
Native of this province		−0.701***	−0.665***	−0.009	−0.665***	−0.009
		(0.195)	(0.229)	(0.284)	(0.187)	(0.252)
College degree		−0.591**	−0.664**	−0.595*	−0.664**	−0.595**
		(0.238)	(0.268)	(0.325)	(0.274)	(0.272)
Postgraduate degree		−0.942***	−1.214***	−1.168**	−1.214***	−1.168***
		(0.342)	(0.398)	(0.459)	(0.392)	(0.389)
With on-the-job degree		−0.184	−0.142	−0.145	−0.142	−0.145
		(0.239)	(0.274)	(0.315)	(0.289)	(0.318)

Table 7 (cont.)

	DV: Promotion					
Variables	**(1) Full**	**(2) Full**	**(3) Full**	**(4) W/O DPS**	**(5) Full**	**(6) W/O DPS**
Years of tenure		0.243	0.357**	0.321	0.357**	0.321
		(0.150)	(0.179)	(0.203)	(0.143)	(0.215)
Professional title		−0.317	−0.171	−0.109	−0.171	−0.109
		(0.210)	(0.239)	(0.270)	(0.276)	(0.316)
Age^2		−0.036***	−0.045***	−0.049***	−0.045***	−0.049***
		(0.008)	(0.010)	(0.011)	(0.015)	(0.017)
Years of $tenure^2$		−0.019	−0.024	−0.019	−0.024**	−0.019
		(0.013)	(0.015)	(0.017)	(0.012)	(0.021)
Connected to prov. party sec.		0.157	0.463	0.428	0.463*	0.428
		(0.256)	(0.297)	(0.335)	(0.250)	(0.294)
Connected to prov. governor		−0.258	−0.137	−0.093	−0.137	−0.093
		(0.259)	(0.301)	(0.341)	(0.302)	(0.359)
Province FE	NO	NO	YES	YES	YES	YES
Year FE	NO	NO	YES	YES	YES	YES
Observations	877	644	644	567	644	567

Standard errors are reported in parentheses for columns 1–4, and clustered standard errors at the provincial level are reported in parentheses for columns 5 and 6.

FE = Fixed effects.

*** $p < 0.01$, ** $p < 0.05$, * $p < 0.1$.

Table 8 Explaining promotion of provincial department heads using Baidu Index score

	DV: Promotion					
Variables	**(1) Full**	**(2) Full**	**(3) Full**	**(4) W/O DPS**	**(5) Full**	**(6) W/O DPS**
Baidu Index score	0.188**	0.281***	0.418**	0.520**	0.418*	0.520**
	(0.083)	(0.105)	(0.203)	(0.238)	(0.248)	(0.259)
Age		4.488***	6.403***	6.943***	6.403***	6.943***
		(0.988)	(1.287)	(1.421)	(1.366)	(1.601)
Gender (Female = 1)		0.169	0.171	0.153	0.171	0.153
		(0.419)	(0.515)	(0.518)	(0.527)	(0.578)
Han ethnicity		−0.402	0.393	0.232	0.393	0.232
		(0.341)	(0.450)	(0.481)	(0.356)	(0.378)
Native of this province		−0.732***	−0.751***	−0.658**	−0.751***	−0.658***
		(0.205)	(0.257)	(0.302)	(0.217)	(0.246)
College degree		−0.509**	−0.557*	−0.561	−0.557**	−0.561**
		(0.250)	(0.300)	(0.346)	(0.236)	(0.268)
Postgraduate degree		−1.105***	−1.262***	−1.140**	−1.262***	−1.140***
		(0.364)	(0.430)	(0.484)	(0.354)	(0.351)
On-the-job education		0.069	0.314	0.277	0.314	0.277
		(0.259)	(0.326)	(0.367)	(0.330)	(0.324)

Table 8 (cont.)

	DV: Promotion					
Variables	**(1) Full**	**(2) Full**	**(3) Full**	**(4) W/O DPS**	**(5) Full**	**(6) W/O DPS**
Years of tenure		0.325*	0.394**	0.330	0.394**	0.330
		(0.173)	(0.198)	(0.209)	(0.179)	(0.208)
Professional title		−0.031	0.282	0.347	0.282	0.347
		(0.209)	(0.252)	(0.282)	(0.277)	(0.297)
Age^2		−0.043***	−0.061***	−0.066***	−0.061***	−0.066***
		(0.009)	(0.012)	(0.013)	(0.013)	(0.015)
Years of $tenure^2$		−0.033**	−0.035**	−0.032*	−0.035**	−0.032
		(0.016)	(0.018)	(0.019)	(0.017)	(0.020)
Connected to prov. party sec.		0.021	0.286	0.214	0.286	0.214
		(0.264)	(0.311)	(0.343)	(0.309)	(0.329)
Connected to prov. governor		−0.154	−0.013	0.082	−0.013	0.082
		(0.260)	(0.316)	(0.343)	(0.277)	(0.306)
Province FE	NO	NO	YES	YES	YES	YES
Year FE	NO	NO	YES	YES	YES	YES
Observations	772	568	568	505	568	505

Standard errors are reported in parentheses for columns 1–4, and clustered standard errors at the provincial level are reported in parentheses for columns 5 and 6.

FE = Fixed effects.

*** $p < 0.01$, ** $p < 0.05$, * $p < 0.1$.

Department heads and runs the full specification. As discussed in Section 3.2, the rationale for excluding Public Security Department is primarily due to significant differences in the two measurements for the key explanatory variable and because the concurrent appointment of Public Security Department heads as deputy provincial officials is more a convention than a promotion. Models 5 and 6 report the results after clustering the standard errors at the provincial level for Models 3 and 4, respectively.

The regression results show that the relevance index is consistently a positive and significant predictor for promotion across all models. The more frequently keywords related to a provincial department's core function are mentioned in the government work report, the more likely the department's head is to be promoted. The Baidu Index score also shows a positive and significant coefficient in different models. This indicates that departments with higher public search frequency are similarly more likely to have their heads promoted. These results highlight the impact of securing superior attention on the career advancement of department heads. Both the government work report relevance index, which directly reflects the attention allocation of provincial party and government leaders, and the Baidu Index, which measures trending social issues indirectly influencing leaders' attention allocation, are positively correlated with the promotion of provincial department leaders.

Among other variables, age and education are two significant predictors. The age variable is positively significant, while its squared term is negatively significant. These results indicate that while more experienced cadres have an advantage in promotions, those who are too old (e.g., approaching the statutory retirement age) may no longer be considered for promotion. Additionally, the variables for having a college degree or a postgraduate degree are unexpectedly negatively significant. This finding appears to contradict existing literature emphasizing the CPC's focus on building a professionalized cadre team. We argue that this result precisely reflects the appointment logic for the specific group of department heads. Cadres with highly specialized professional training (e.g., medical professionals or financial experts with postgraduate degrees) are more likely to serve long term in functional departments (or be laterally transferred to other department-level positions) rather than being promoted to deputy provincial-level positions or appointed as party secretaries of prefecture-level cities.[45] Additionally, whether a cadre was born in the province shows

[45] For cadres who served as department heads around 2010 (typically in their 50s), their full-time education took place in the 1980s. At that time, a university bachelor's degree was extremely rare, let alone a graduate degree. Many cadres entering government departments had only a high school or vocational college education (associate degree) as their first degree, compensating for this educational gap later in their careers through part-time or continuing education programs.

a significant negative correlation in most models. While local networks may aid a cadre's early career development, senior leaders, when appointing provincial leaders or municipal party secretaries, may prefer to avoid appointing local cadres to reduce corruption and achieve other governance objectives (e.g., Jia & Nie, 2017).

As already mentioned, eight provincial departments have data for both measurements, allowing us to compare the impact of the two metrics. Table 9 presents the regression results that simultaneously include the relevance index and the Baidu Index score. The results show that the relevance index consistently demonstrates significance across all models, while the Baidu Index results are no longer as significant as in Table 8. Although this finding is based on a reduced sample, it suggests that the direct mechanism may be more effective than the indirect one. When a department's work directly aligns with the medium- to long-term policy priorities of superiors, its head receives consistent attention from their superiors and is therefore more likely to get promoted.

We also conducted a series of robustness checks. First, in the baseline model, we coded promotion as 1 and all other outcomes (i.e., lateral transfer, retirement, or investigation) as 0. Following Landry, Lü, and Duan (2018, p. 1085), in the robustness checks, we coded promotion as 1, lateral transfer as 0, and excluded observations with other outcomes, yielding results similar to the baseline models. We also replaced the logistic regression in the baseline models with the linear probability model employed by Landry, Lü, and Duan (2018). Additionally, while the baseline model used the connection measurement from the last year of a department head's tenure, in the robustness checks, we used the average connections with the provincial party secretary and governor during the department head's tenure. We also used alternative coding scheme for the education variable (as an ordinal variable). Results from these additional analyses were consistent with those of the baseline models. Finally, in the baseline models our unit of analysis is department head, and we also used annual data in the robustness checks. While the results with the Baidu Index score as the key explanatory variable lost statistical significance in the full model specification, the results with the relevance index as the key explanatory variable were consistent with those in the baseline models. Due to space constraints, we do not report all these results individually.

3.5 Career Advancement within the MFA: A Case Study

We test the external validity of our argument by further examining the career development patterns of department leaders within the MFA. Unlike many other State Council ministries, the foreign ministry is a highly insular professional

Table 9 Comparing the two measures

	DV: Promotion					
Variables	**(1) Full**	**(2) Full**	**(3) Full**	**(4) W/O DPS**	**(5) Full**	**(6) W/O DPS**
Relevance index	0.084	0.301***	0.391***	1.052***	0.391***	1.052***
	(0.083)	(0.110)	(0.141)	(0.240)	(0.141)	(0.232)
Baidu Index score	0.136	0.206*	0.425*	−0.307	0.425	−0.307
	(0.089)	(0.113)	(0.240)	(0.367)	(0.264)	(0.338)
Control variables	NO	YES	YES	YES	YES	YES
Province FE	NO	NO	YES	YES	YES	YES
Year FE	NO	NO	YES	YES	YES	YES
Observations	602	442	442	379	442	379

Standard errors are reported in parentheses for columns 1–4, and clustered standard errors at the provincial level are reported in parentheses for columns 5 and 6. The control variables are the same as those in Tables 7 and 8.

FE = Fixed effects.

*** $p < 0.01$, ** $p < 0.05$, * $p < 0.1$.

system. According to our statistics, from 1978 to 2024, 65.45% of MFA leaders (including ministers, vice ministers, assistant ministers, and members of the ministry's party committee) worked in the MFA from their first job, and almost all of them (94.05%) held their immediate prior position within the MFA before becoming ministerial leaders. This insularity reduces interference from external transfers on promotions, and allows us to better compare promotion probabilities across different internal departments.[46]

Eligible candidates for leadership positions in the MFA primarily fall into two categories (Jost & Li, 2025). The first category includes cadres serving as directors of the MFA's internal departments. The MFA currently has twenty-nine internal departments, including functional departments such as the General Office, Information Department, Protocol Department, and Personnel Department, as well as regional departments responsible for specific areas, such as the Department of Asian Affairs, Department of European Affairs, and Department of North American and Oceanian Affairs.[47] The second category comprises diplomats serving as ambassadors to other countries and international organizations.[48] This distinction is akin to the difference between "*tiao*" (functional departments) and "*kuai*" (territorial administrations) commonly seen in the Chinese bureaucratic system. According to our data, since 1949, among all MFA leaders, 51.79% held their immediate prior position as an ambassador abroad, 37.5% were heads of internal MFA bureaus, and the remaining 10.71% came from outside of the ministry.[49] Existing research finds that diplomats who work in Beijing (i.e., internal bureaus) generally enjoy an advantage in promotion than those who spend their careers in postings abroad (Jost & Li, 2025).

In this case study, we focus on identifying which heads of internal bureaus are more likely to be promoted to MFA leadership. Since MFA leaders are centrally managed cadres, their appointment and removal are decided by the central leadership of the CPC. We collected the career histories of all cadres who

[46] In contrast, among those promoted to provincial leaders or municipal party secretaries at the prefecture level, many come from roles beyond provincial department heads.

[47] For a list of current MFA bureaus, visit www.mfa.gov.cn/web/wjb_673085/zzjg_673183/, last accessed May 6, 2025.

[48] Ambassadors to the United States, Russia, France, the United Kingdom, Germany, Japan, North Korea, the United Nations, and a few other countries and international organizations hold vice-ministerial ranks, and their transfer to roles such as vice minister or member of the ministry's party committee is considered a lateral move rather than a promotion.

[49] These cadres transferred from outside mainly come from relevant foreign affairs departments such as the Ministry of Commerce, the Party's International Liaison Department, and the Foreign Affairs Office of the CPC Central Committee. Additionally, in the early years of the People's Republic, some MFA leaders were also transferred from the People's Liberation Army, intelligence agencies, and other institutions.

eventually became MFA leaders, including their positions before assuming leadership roles. Through descriptive statistical analysis, we examined which heads of internal departments of MFA were more likely to become ministry leaders. Without presupposing theoretical hypotheses, the probability of department heads becoming ministry leaders should follow a uniform distribution (i.e., the likelihood of capable cadres emerging from each department and being recognized and promoted by superiors should be roughly equal). As our data span seventy-five years (1949–2024), covering numerous heads for each department, the resulting patterns are more likely to reflect relatively stable departmental characteristics rather than shifting priorities of superiors or personal idiosyncrasies of departmental leaders. If certain departments have a significantly higher probability of their heads becoming ministry leaders compared to others, it suggests implicit differences among these departments despite their identical administrative ranks. We will focus on analyzing the characteristics of these implicit "stepping stone" departments for career advancement, particularly whether these departments have an advantage over others in gaining the attention of the party's central leadership.

Figure 6 shows the sixteen departments with at least one head becoming MFA leader, with data provided for the period 1949–2024. Table 10 lists the full names of these departments and their corresponding abbreviations used in Figure 6.

Several clear patterns emerge from this comparison. The likelihood of heads of twenty-nine MFA departments becoming ministry leaders varies significantly. Only sixteen departments have had at least one head promoted to MFA

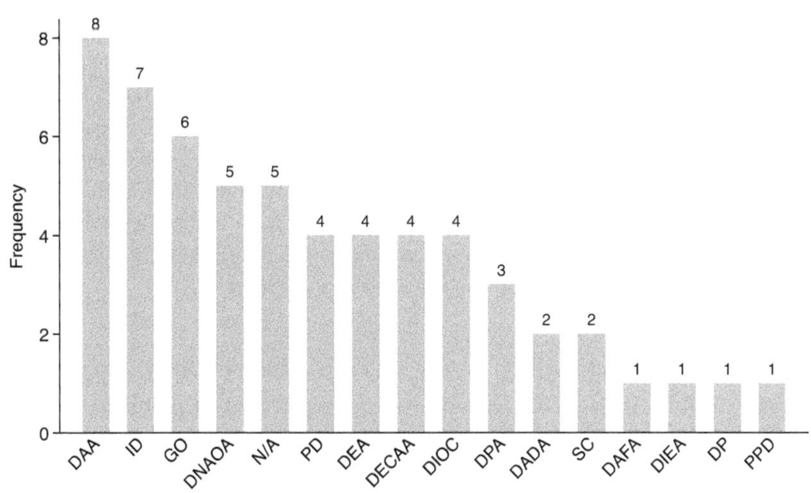

Figure 6 Immediate previous positions of MFA leaders.

Table 10 List of MFA departments in Figure 6

Official English name[a]	Chinese name	Abbreviation
Department of Asian Affairs	亚洲司	DAA
Information Department	新闻司	ID
General Office	办公厅	GO
Other[b]	其他	N/A
Department of North American and Oceanian Affairs	北美大洋洲司	DNAOA
Protocol Department	礼宾司	PD
Department of International Organizations and Conferences	国际司	DIOC
Department of European-Central Asian Affairs	欧亚司	DECAA
Department of European Affairs	欧洲司	DEA
Department of Party Affairs	机关党委（部党委国外工作局）	DPA
Service Center	服务中心	SC
Department of Administrative Affairs	行政司	DADA
Policy Planning Department	政策规划司	PPD
Department of Personnel	干部司	DP
Department of International Economic Affairs	国际经济司	DIEA
Department of African Affairs	非洲司	DAFA

Notes:

a. If the name of a department has changed, we use the latest department name.

b. This category contains two departments: Department of West Asian and North African Affairs (WANAA) and Department of Western European, North American and Oceanian Affairs (WENAOA). Both departments underwent major reorganization in history. The WANAA used to encompass African affairs (which now becomes an independent department) between 1956 and 1964, and 1969 and 1972. The WENAOA was abolished in 1972 and became Department of Western European Affairs, a predecessor to present-day DEA, and DNAOA. For the sake of simplicity, we categorize these two departments into "other."

leadership throughout the PRC history.[50] Leading the pack are the Department of Asian Affairs, Information Department, General Office, Department of North

50 Even when including vice-ministerial level ambassadors, only nineteen departments have had directors general promoted to vice-ministerial roles in the MFA, with the additional three being the Department of Arms Control, Department of External Security Affairs, and Department of Treaty and Law.

American and Oceanian Affairs, and Protocol Department. The top five departments account for 53.4% of all ministry leaders promoted from department head positions. Some traditionally important functional departments (e.g., Personnel) are on the list but rank relatively low.[51] Among the higher-ranked departments, there are both functional departments (e.g., Information and Protocol) and those responsible for specific regional diplomatic affairs (e.g., Asian, North American, and Oceanian). In the analysis, we will demonstrate that their common characteristic is that the nature of their respective duties makes it easier for them to gain the attention of central leadership.

Take the top-ranked Department of Asian Affairs as an example. Its responsibilities cover most of China's fourteen land neighbors and six maritime neighbors.[52] China maintains close relations with these neighbors, being the largest trading partner for most of them, resolving historical border issues through negotiations, and establishing partnerships, cooperative relations, or strategic mutually beneficial relationships.[53] When heads of state or government from these countries visit China, or when Chinese leaders visit these nations, the head of the Department of Asian Affairs is routinely required to accompany them. In fact, according to official documents, China "has always placed its neighborhood as the top priority in its overall diplomacy."[54] At the Central Committee level, in addition to the Central Conference on Foreign Affairs, there is a dedicated Central Conference on Neighborhood Affairs, underscoring its special status. Beyond managing relations with neighboring countries, the Department of Asian Affairs is also responsible for a large number of regional organizations and cooperative mechanisms, such as Association of Southeast Asian Nations, China–Japan–South Korea Cooperation, the East Asia Summit, Lancang–Mekong Cooperation, and the Six-Party Talks on the North Korean nuclear issue, in which Chinese national leaders regularly participate. As a result, the department's head gains numerous opportunities to accompany national leaders on visits or report directly to them.

The mechanism of the Department of North American and Oceanian Affairs is similar to that of the Department of Asian Affairs.[55] Its responsibilities include managing relations with the United States, which is considered China's most

---

[51] In comparison, almost all former heads of the Ministry of Education's Personnel Department in recent decades have been promoted to ministry leadership or university leadership roles with vice-ministerial rank.

[52] A few former Soviet republics, such as Russia and Central Asian countries, are managed by the Department of European-Central Asian Affairs.

[53] See Gov.cn, Outlook on China's Neighborhood Diplomacy Policy in the New Era (Full Text), [in Chinese], www.gov.cn/yaowen/liebiao/202310/content_6911402.htm, last accessed May 8, 2025.

[54] Ibid.

[55] So are the mechanisms for the Department of European Affairs and the Department of International Organizations and Conferences.

important bilateral relationship, directly overseen by the paramount leader. As a result, the head of this department has numerous opportunities to interact directly with the country's top leadership. The Protocol Department, primarily responsible for ceremonial and logistical matters, differs significantly in its scope of work from the Asian and North American and Oceanian Affairs Departments. However, the mechanism by which its leaders regularly secure promotions is similar. The head of the Protocol Department is required to closely accompany and serve national leaders (the President and the Premier in particular) during significant diplomatic events, thereby securing substantial "face time" with them.[56] A prominent recent example is Qin Gang, who, as the head of the Protocol Department before his promotion to a leadership role in the MFA, was frequently seen directly supporting Chinese national leaders at key diplomatic events. The promotion pathway for leaders in the General Office is similarly structured. As a department responsible for coordinating internal ministerial affairs, the General Office primarily supports the MFA's top leadership. The Foreign Minister, often concurrently holding a senior national role (such as State Councilor or Politburo member), wields considerable influence in nominating deputy positions within the ministry. Consequently, the head of the General Office gains a distinct career advantage through frequent visibility and direct interaction with the minister. In summary, despite the vastly different operational scopes of these departments, their leaders all have ample opportunities to *directly* gain the attention of senior leaders who can influence their career advancement.

The Information Department ranks second among all departments. Its primary responsibilities include "disseminating information on China's major diplomatic activities, articulating China's foreign policy," and managing "foreign news organizations and journalists stationed in China."[57] Compared to the departments analyzed earlier, the Information Department has fewer opportunities for direct interaction with central leadership. However, it serves as the public face of the MFA. The general public's understanding of China's diplomatic policies and activities largely stems from the department's regular press conferences, where the department head also serves as one of the spokespersons. Many trending social media stories related to diplomacy originate from the spokespersons' remarks at these briefings, and numerous MFA spokespersons have even become household names.[58] It is no exaggeration to say that the head of the Information

[56] See People.com "Ministry of Foreign Affairs Protocol Department: Zero Distance from Historic Events" [in Chinese] http://paper.people.com.cn/zgjjzk/html/2013-12/16/content_1363786.htm, last accessed May 10, 2025.

[57] For an official description of the department's responsibility, see www.mfa.gov.cn/web/wjb_673085/zzjg_673183/xws_674681/, last accessed May 10, 2025.

[58] A prominent example is Zhao Lijian, known domestically and internationally for his "wolf warrior" style of rhetoric.

Department enjoys the highest public visibility among all MFA department heads. As illustrated in the earlier analysis of provincial government functional departments, matters or individuals with high public recognition or attention are often channeled back to senior leadership, influencing their focus and decision-making. Leaders of the Information Department, therefore, through their high public and social visibility, *indirectly* garner the attention of national leaders who can influence their career advancement.

In summary, this section tests the core hypothesis proposed in Section 2: An official's likelihood of promotion, particularly for heads of functional departments where performance is difficult to measure or attribute, largely depends on their ability to capture the attention of superiors. A common critique contends that leaders of certain departments are promoted more often simply because those departments are inherently "important," and that cadres placed in such posts – often trusted protégés – are therefore better positioned for leadership. I address this critique in several ways. First, what counts as "important" is highly subjective and often defined ex post: any department can justify its significance from its remit, and many reputations for importance arise because numerous officials from those units were later promoted. This section offers an empirical mechanism behind such perceptions: a department head's capacity to secure attention – directly or indirectly – shapes the department's perceived importance, which in turn influences the head's career prospects. Second, even among traditionally "important" departments, their heads do not necessarily enjoy higher promotion odds than counterparts in ostensibly less important units that, for various reasons, are more visible to superiors. The case study of the MFA shows that heads of the Personnel Department are less likely to be promoted than heads of seemingly more peripheral units such as Protocol.[59] Third, salience is fluid. Previously marginal departments can become leadership priorities during exogenous shocks, temporarily boosting their leaders' promotion chances – for example, local public health departments during the pandemic.[60] Last but not the least, as discussed in Section 2.3, the number of trusted confidants a leader can rely on is typically far smaller than the number of appointments they must make; for the vast majority of posts, leaders therefore need other ways to identify suitable candidates.

---

[59] The peripheral position of the protocol unit in other country's diplomatic bureaucracy is also corroborated by interview with a retired staff of the US State Department on February 20, 2025.

[60] For example, Zhang Ping, the director of Zhejiang Provincial Health Commission between 2018 and 2022, was promoted to serve as the chairman of Ningbo's Municipal People's Congress Standing Committee, a deputy provincial-level position, in 2022. He became the first director of that province's Health Commission to be directly promoted to a deputy provincial-level position.

As shown in the MFA case, the ability to capture attention is certainly shaped by the department's inherent responsibilities, but it can also be influenced by public opinion, unexpected events, or shifts in the policy priorities of senior leaders, as well as by the actions of the department heads themselves. In the next section, we will focus on analyzing the potential impact of proactive behaviors by subordinate leaders to gain the attention of superiors on governance performance.

4 Attention and Bureaucratic Pathologies

One challenge facing the political meritocracy thesis is why, in a system that claims to rationally select and promote capable officials, there are still numerous instances of bureaucratic behaviors that deviate from the governance objectives expected by superiors. These behaviors include, but are not limited to, non-implementation or selective implementation of policies prioritized by superiors; or, at the other extreme, overly zealous implementation that may produce counterproductive results; while some officials merely engage in performative compliance to superficially address tasks assigned by superiors. Such bureaucratic pathologies exist at all levels and have persisted throughout the CPC's revolutionary and state-building periods. Their prevalence and persistence suggest the presence of systemic, institutional factors (beyond individual officials' characteristics) contributing to these phenomena.[61] This section continues to analyze, through the lens of attention, how subordinates' efforts to gain recognition (attention) from superiors or to evade accountability in an environment where performance measurement is challenging ultimately lead to the aforementioned bureaucratic pathologies.

4.1 Anti-Bureaucratism in CPC History

From its inception, the CPC has been deeply marked by a strong anti-bureaucratism stance. Ding and Thompson-Brusstar (2021) point out that, as a revolutionary party born in the historical context of the collapse of a feudal bureaucratic society, the CPC has an inherent vigilance toward the bureaucratic elite and bureaucratic tendencies that stand in opposition to the people. Although this tendency has persisted through the CPC's revolutionary period and its state-building and development phases, the specific phenomena denoted by the term "bureaucratism" have varied across different periods. In the early revolutionary period, Mao Zedong used "bureaucratism" to describe officials from the old society who put on airs, avoided contact with the masses, and acted superior

[61] For existing discussions on how the cadre evaluation system contributes to various bureaucratic pathologies, see, for example, Gao (2015, 2021).

(Mao, 1930). Liu Shaoqi (1939) used historical examples to warn CPC members against becoming bureaucratic after achieving victory, losing their revolutionary spirit, and turning against the people (i.e., becoming new exploiters).

After the founding of the People's Republic of China in 1949, due to the needs of governing the country, the CPC, with its core mission of opposing bureaucratism, was forced to coexist with bureaucratic systems. During this period, in addition to the meanings accumulated during the revolutionary period, bureaucratism took on new connotations related to the challenges faced by the ruling party. In his article "Opposing Bureaucratism," Zhou Enlai (1963) outlined twenty specific manifestations of bureaucratism, most of which were related to redundancies and inefficiencies in bureaucratic operations, such as bloated institutions (*jigou pangza*), excessive meetings (*huiyiduo*), exaggeration and concealment (*fukua manbao*), and perfunctory handling of issues (*yushi fuyan*). Many scholars argue that a key objective of the series of political campaigns launched by Mao in the 1950s and 1960s, including the Cultural Revolution, was to eradicate the bureaucratic tendencies within the CPC (e.g., Whyte, 1973).

During the reform and opening-up period, the ideological fervor of the Mao era gradually diminished, and the rationalization and professionalization of the bureaucracy increased (e.g., Pieke, 2009). However, tensions between the Leninist party structure and the professionalized bureaucratic system persisted. For instance, the CPC continued to use various "managed campaigns" to rectify the bureaucratic system and achieve governance objectives (Perry, 2011). In recent decades, the concept of bureaucratism has almost always been paired with formalism (*xingshi zhuyi*) in policy documents (Ding & Thompson-Brusstar, 2021). Bureaucratism and formalism have also become an umbrella term used to refer to various phenomena that deviate from the ideal principal–agent relationship, encompassing officials' work attitudes, implementation methods, and ultimate outcomes.[62] Although the Party Central Committee has repeatedly issued directives and launched campaigns to curb formalism and bureaucratism, these phenomena have not disappeared and continue to exhibit considerable prevalence and persistence.[63] The analysis below seeks to demonstrate that the existence of these bureaucratic pathologies is not a product of

[62] For example, see Gov.cn, "Notice on Continuously Addressing Formalism Issues Troubling the Grassroots to Provide a Strong Work Style Guarantee for Comprehensively Achieving a Moderately Prosperous Society" [in Chinese], www.gov.cn/zhengce/2020-04/14/content_5502349.htm, last accessed May 25, 2025.

[63] For example, during the COVID-19 prevention and control efforts, the Standing Committee of the Political Bureau of the CPC Central Committee addressed the need to oppose formalism and bureaucratism on multiple occasions, including meetings in February 2020 and November 2022. For the February 2020 meeting, see www.gov.cn/xinwen/2020-02/03/content_5474309.htm; for the November 2022 meeting, see www.xinhuanet.com/politics/2022-11/10/c_1129118595.htm, both last accessed May 27, 2025.

individual officials' moral failings but rather a result of the incentive structures inherent in a top-down bureaucratic system.

4.2 A Typology of Bureaucratic Behaviors

For officials across different departments, regions, and responsibilities, while they enjoy a certain level of discretion in policy implementation, they all operate within a top-down bureaucratic system where senior leaders determine subordinates' career advancement and resource allocation among subdivisions (Harding, 1981).[64] As the saying goes: "One is accountable to those who grant power." Consequently, the policy objectives of one's direct superiors and their corresponding incentive mechanisms become critical factors in shaping subordinates' behaviors (e.g., O'Brien & Li, 1999). In our analytical framework, we use two dimensions – the clarity with which senior leaders' policy intent can be translated into assessments criteria and the specific incentive methods superiors adopt – to construct an analytical typology of bureaucratic behaviors (Ma & Ma, 2021).

The first dimension of our analysis is the clarity of superiors' policy intent. Specifically, this refers to the extent to which the goals that superiors expect subordinates to achieve can be reflected through clear evaluation metrics. This dimension is closely related to the measurability and attributability of performance discussed in Section 2. For some policy objectives, such as attracting investment or fiscal revenue collection, the policy goals of superiors can be easily measured with objective numerical indicators. Subordinates in these areas can easily gain the attention of superiors by diligently performing their responsibilities. However, some other policy objectives, such as party building and clean governance, spiritual civilization construction, or public security, are more difficult to measure directly with numbers. For security-related goals, for example, using metrics like the number of cases cannot accurately reflect governance performance. A recent example is in Liaoning Province's drug enforcement management, where the provincial authority used the number of drug-related crime crackdowns as an evaluation metric, resulting in some counties with effective drug control being unable to meet the targets due to a lack of drug-related crimes. This even led to a few anti-drug officers colluding with drug trafficking organizations to smuggle drugs, solely to meet the superiors' task objectives.[65] In Wilson (1989)'s study of the American bureaucracy, he terms such security-related departments as "coping agencies" and highlights the difficulties in measuring their performance.

---

[64] This section is based on analysis in Ma & Ma (2021).

[65] See *Southern Weekly*, "Turning drug dealers into informants, anti-drug police accused of drug smuggling" [in Chinese] https://mp.weixin.qq.com/s/Hdb9psZYrTwvmdo61y7tyw, last accessed May 14, 2025.

For departments where work outputs are hard to quantify, superiors may resort to inputs-based evaluation (e.g., Kerr, 1975; Jensen & Meckling, 1976; Ouchi, 1979). For instance, the evaluation of foreign affairs departments at various levels often relies on metrics such as the number of events organized or the number of internal reference reports submitted.[66] Compared to issue areas where evaluations are directly based on outputs, such input-based assessments have lower clarity. For some opportunistic officials, strategically increasing the visibility of inputs can also gain the approval of superiors without regard for the actual effectiveness of their work.

The second dimension of our analysis is the incentive mechanism employed by superiors toward subordinates. This dimension encompasses two forms: positive incentives and negative incentives. Positive incentives involve rewarding officials who meet superior objectives, with specific forms including promotions, salary increases, or honorary recognitions. Under positive incentives, officials who perform poorly in evaluations may not receive rewards but retain their current status. Negative incentives involve punishing officials who fail to meet performance targets, with measures such as demotion, dismissal, public criticism, or salary reductions. Under negative incentives, officials who meet targets typically receive no additional rewards. Subordinate officials have different goals under different incentives. Under positive incentives, their goal is to excel (perform better than peers), while under negative incentives, their primary goal is to avoid accountability (not falling behind or making mistakes). The type of incentive mechanism adopted by superiors often depends on the specific task and context. For developmental metrics, such as economic growth or cultural development, positive incentives are typically used, while for control-oriented metrics (i.e., mandatory tasks), such as environmental protection or social stability, negative incentives are more common. Of course, superiors can flexibly adjust the incentive type based on immediate needs. For example, during an economic downturn, goals like attracting investment may be disaggregated among subordinates, with negative incentives (punishments) applied to those who fail to meet them, rather than the positive incentives more commonly used for such metrics in normal times. It should be noted that these incentive mechanisms can be applied both to the evaluation of whether task objectives are achieved and to the process of achieving those objectives. When an official intentionally or unintentionally commits mistakes during the implementation of a policy goal, even if the goal is achieved, the superior can still hold them accountable.

[66] Interviews with a staff member from the Overseas Chinese Affairs Office of the State Council, July 2, 2022, and a staff member from the Foreign Affairs Office of Shandong Province, May 11, 2025.

Table 11 A typology of bureaucratic behaviors

		Incentive types	
		Negative	**Positive**
Clarity of superior's policy intention	**Low**	Non-implementation	Performative implementation
	High	Over-implementation	Active implementation

Based on these two dimensions, we can construct a two-by-two table to explain officials' behaviors, as shown in Table 11. The four quadrants in the table correspond to four common bureaucratic behaviors: "non-implementation," "over-implementation," "performative implementation," and "active implementation." All types except active implementation represent some form of deviation or distortion from the policy intentions of superiors. Additionally, these four behavioral types are ideal types based on the characteristics of a single policy goal. In reality, an official may be required to achieve multiple policy goals simultaneously, and thus may exhibit a combination of behaviors. For example, when non-implementation coexists with over-implementation or active implementation, it constitutes the typical "selective implementation" (O'Brien & Li, 1999).[67]

Non-implementation refers to subordinates adopting a passive strategy toward tasks assigned by superiors, manifested by not taking additional actions. When a superior's policy goals cannot be clearly measured with definitive indicators, and local officials face high risks in implementing these policies, where any issues could easily lead to punishment, local officials are likely to adopt a strategy of non-implementation. This phenomenon is described in Chinese with terms such as "*buzuowei*" (inaction) or "*weiguan buwei*" (officials doing nothing). For rational officials, the immeasurability of the superior's intent makes the consequences of inaction difficult for superiors to detect, with limited risk. In contrast, proactive action may bring additional accountability risks.

[67] Some scholars have proposed other typologies of bureaucratic behaviors. For example, Ding (2020) categorizes the behavior of local government departments into four types – inert, paternalistic, performative, and substantive – based on the dimensions of capacity and scrutiny. Liu (2021) proposes a typology of policing behaviors (i.e., deceptive/superficial, zealous, lazy, and selective) by looking at individual incentive and political pressure. Ding and van der Kamp (2024) propose four types of policy implementation in the context of environmental policy, based on the dimensions of start-up costs and maintenance costs: symbolic implementation, sporadic implementation, over-implementation, and consistent implementation.

In various reports issued by the party's Commission for Discipline Inspection regarding non-implementation behaviors, a common case involves grassroots (e.g., township) cadres failing to promptly address "dual violations" (illegal land use and illegal construction) in building construction.[68] For the state, cracking down on such violations is crucial for regulating land management and ensuring building safety. However, unlike in large cities, illegal constructions in rural and peri-urban areas are difficult to detect. Typically, such buildings are only identified through proactive public tip-offs (*jubao*), followed by on-site investigations by higher authorities. In the absence of reports, expecting township governments to allocate resources from their numerous busy tasks to regularly inspect for illegal constructions is impractical. On the other hand, once illegal buildings are identified and require demolition, township governments may face numerous compensation and legal challenges, and affected parties might resort to extreme measures (e.g., petitions or protests) that threaten social stability. If mishandled, resulting in negative social impacts, the responsible officials may face punishment. Therefore, rational grassroots officials often turn a blind eye to illegal constructions, leading to the occurrence of non-implementation.

Performative implementation refers to a ceremonial response strategy adopted by subordinates toward tasks assigned by superiors. Unlike non-implementation, these officials often display an active attitude in addressing superior tasks, but the actual impact of their actions falls far short of the superiors' intention. When the policy goals of superiors cannot be clearly measured with indicators, and the actions taken by officials to implement these policies carry little risk or even offer rewards, performative implementation is likely to occur. Since policy goals (i.e., outputs) cannot be clearly measured, superiors' evaluations of subordinates might rely on indirect, input-based indicators. This encourages subordinates to invest effort and resources in areas observable by superiors to gain rewards, without much concern for the actual effectiveness of these actions, as superiors are also unable to measure outcomes clearly.

A typical example of performative implementation is *wenshan huihai* (a mountain of documents and a sea of meetings). For any field of work, documents and meetings are necessary, but when their quantity and frequency exceed what is required, they constitute formalism. This phenomenon is particularly prevalent in the implementation of superiors' directives (*luoshi shangji zhishi*), especially for tasks that are difficult to quantify, such as spiritual

[68] For example, see Sohu.com. "Shanwei Vigorously Rectifies 'Official Inaction,' Publicizing 5 Typical Cases" [in Chinese] www.sohu.com/a/80501597_222493, last accessed May 15, 2025.

civilization construction. When superiors require substantive work to be carried out, subordinates respond by issuing documents or holding meetings.[69] In Chinese officialdom, this has given rise to the saying: "using meetings to implement meetings, using documents to implement documents." Often, whether subordinates truly grasp the intentions of superiors is difficult to assess objectively. By issuing documents or holding meetings – which are visible actions – subordinates demonstrate to superiors their efforts to align with those intentions, a typical strategic behavior under an input-based evaluation system. Compared to non-implementation, this scenario does not entail severe punishment for those who fail to perform well (while subordinates who demonstrate efforts or good work ethics may receive rewards). Moreover, organizing meetings or issuing documents poses relatively low and controllable risks for subordinates, with no danger of being held accountable for unintended failures. Additionally, local officials' construction of "image projects" (*xingxiang gongcheng*) or "face-saving projects" (*mianzi gongcheng*) also falls within the scope of performative implementation. Lacking the willingness or ability to fully realize superiors' intentions, local officials are incentivized to undertake a few high-visibility projects to showcase achievements and superficially satisfy superiors.[70] Whether it is "*wenshan huihai*" or "image projects," both point to the core issue in the evaluation system: superiors' inability to clearly assess the effectiveness of subordinates' policy implementation.

Over-implementation refers to the use of extreme measures to carry out superiors' policy goals, often resulting in deviations from the true objectives or causing significant negative impacts on other goals. In the Chinese context, such behaviors are often described as "*yidaoqie*" (one-size-fits-all) or "*cengceng jiama*" (layer-upon-layer escalation). Over-implementation typically occurs in areas where policy goals can be clearly measured and where officials who fail to meet these goals face severe accountability. Since the task objectives are clearly measurable, subordinate officials cannot resort to "non-implementation" or "performative implementation" to cope. To avoid punishment, subordinates often adopt one of two approaches: one is to mechanically execute superiors' directives without adapting to local realities, a "one-size-fits-all" approach that shifts responsibility back to superiors; the other is to

[69] For typical examples, see "Notice on Forwarding Reports Regarding Two Typical Cases of Addressing Formalism to Reduce Burdens on Grassroots Levels in Certain Regions" [in Chinese] www.xcs.gov.cn/content/detail/67242e2f6803fa658d8b456a.html, last accessed May 16, 2025.

[70] For typical examples of image projects, see "The Central Commission for Discipline Inspection and the National Supervisory Commission Publicly Report Six Typical Cases of Formalism and Bureaucratism" [in Chinese] https://baijiahao.baidu.com/s?id=1786425542952524589&wfr=-spider&for=pc, last accessed May 16, 2025.

proactively amplify the execution targets to avoid lagging behind peers and facing accountability, which leads to the phenomenon of "layer-upon-layer escalation."

Environmental protection and epidemic prevention are two areas prone to over-implementation. Whether subordinates have implemented superiors' environmental requirements can be clearly measured through indicators such as energy consumption per unit, pollutant emissions, and PM2.5 levels, or directly observed through phenomena like black and odorous water bodies or smog and dust. Officials who fail to meet these environmental targets often face punishment. In 2016 alone, during the first round of central environmental inspections in eight provinces, 1,140 cadres were held accountable, including 130 at the provincial department level.[71] Local officials have thus adopted numerous extreme measures in environmental governance, such as imposing "one-size-fits-all" forced shutdowns of businesses and enterprises during inspections by superiors, severely disrupting the daily lives and livelihoods of the public. Such unsustainable practices also contradict the original intent of superiors for environmental protection.[72] Similar to environmental protection, the effectiveness of epidemic prevention can be clearly measured by the number of positive cases in a jurisdiction. During the COVID-19 pandemic, numerous local officials were sacked simply because positive cases emerged in their areas.[73] This incentive structure explains why many localities adopted extreme measures, such as welding shut the doors of people returning from high-risk areas or prohibiting enterprises from resuming production.[74] The clear policy goals and negative incentives from superiors made subordinates unwilling to take any risks.

Active implementation is the type of behavior that deviates relatively less from the intentions of superiors among the various types. Under clear evaluation metrics and positive incentives, subordinate cadres proactively adopt methods suited to the characteristics of their jurisdiction to achieve the goals set by superiors. The widely discussed "promotion tournament" based on economic growth (Li & Zhou, 2005) is a typical example of active

[71] See Xinhuanet.com, "First Round of Central Environmental Inspections: 1,140 Individuals Held Accountable Across 8 Provinces" [in Chinese] www.xinhuanet.com/politics/2017-11/17/c_1121968691.htm, last accessed May 16, 2025.

[72] See Beijing Youth Daily, "'One-size-fits-all' Shutdowns Contradict the Original Intent of Environmental Protection" [in Chinese] https://epaper.ynet.com/html/2018-05/29/content_289318.htm?div=-1, last accessed May 16, 2025.

[73] See, for example, Xinhuanet.com, "Three Cadres in Lhasa, Tibet, Were Sacked for Ineffective Epidemic Prevention and Control" [in Chinese] www.news.cn/politics/2022-08/14/c_1128913827.htm, last accessed May 16, 2025.

[74] See, for example, Sohu.com, "Villagers Uncooperative with Epidemic Prevention Had Their Doors Welded Shut by the Village Party Secretary! Local Authorities: Inappropriate" [in Chinese] www.sohu.com/a/514564518_425563, last accessed May 16, 2025.

implementation. On the one hand, the superiors' intent to develop the economy can be clearly measured using GDP growth or other indicators.[75] On the other hand, officials in regions with faster economic growth are promoted, while those in slower-growing regions are not necessarily punished, providing space for localities to explore different development paths based on their endowments. However, this does not mean that implementation under this incentive structure is without issues. For example, the promotion tournament may crowd out other development goals (i.e., see "selective implementation" discussed in the next paragraph) and lead to problems like local protectionism. Additionally, in some special cases, clear goals and strong positive incentives can also result in over-implementation (e.g., Kung & Chen, 2011).

This typology analyzes behaviors within a single policy domain. However, grassroots officials often face multiple task objectives simultaneously across domains such as economy, society, environment, and security, each with distinct characteristics, leading officials to exhibit multiple behavioral types concurrently. When some goals have high clarity while others have low clarity, officials are likely to demonstrate *selective implementation*, actively or even excessively pursuing goals with higher clarity while perfunctorily addressing or ignoring those with lower clarity. O'Brien and Li (1999), in their study of grassroots policy implementation, found that popular policies like "democratic work style," "mass line," and "protecting villagers' autonomous rights" were difficult to measure clearly, resulting in most grassroots officials receiving similar scores in evaluation. In contrast, less socially popular policies like taxation and family planning, which could be clearly quantified, became the primary metrics for distinguishing officials' performance, leading local officials to invest significant effort in their implementation (pp. 173–174).

It should be noted that differences in metric clarity are not only influenced by whether governance goals can be quantified but also by the ease of feedback. Domains where governance performance can be *quickly* assessed tend to be prioritized for implementation. During the COVID-19 pandemic, the central government repeatedly emphasized balancing economic development and epidemic prevention, both relatively easy to quantify.[76] However, many local governments exhibited excessive epidemic prevention at the expense of economic growth. The reason lies in the fact that the effectiveness of epidemic

[75] Some scholars argue that superiors may prioritize maximizing fiscal revenue over GDP growth (e.g., Shih, Adolph, & Liu, 2012; Lü & Landry, 2014).

[76] See, for example, People.com. "'Prevent the epidemic, stabilize the economy, ensure safe development' – A review of General Secretary Xi Jinping's leadership in efficiently coordinating epidemic prevention and control with economic and social development" [in Chinese] http://politics.people.com.cn/n1/2022/0809/c1001-32497620.html, last accessed May 19, 2025.

prevention could be reflected through daily updates on positive case numbers, whereas measurements of economic growth (e.g., GDP growth, fiscal revenue, and employment) have longer cycles (typically reported monthly or quarterly). Additionally, economic growth is often incentivized positively, while epidemic prevention relies on negative incentives. An official genuinely attempting to balance both goals may not have enough time to prove their efforts in sustaining economic growth before being held accountable for inadequate epidemic prevention. This incentive structure ultimately leads rational officials to prioritize epidemic prevention to avoid accountability.

4.3 Empirical Patterns of Bureaucratic Pathologies

The typology in the previous section provides a framework for systematically analyzing bureaucratism and formalism in recent years. Existing empirical studies on bureaucratism and formalism are mostly based on typical case analyses. We attempt to collect and analyze a broader dataset by utilizing relevant cases published on the websites of provincial Party Commissions for Discipline Inspection.

The websites of the Commissions for Discipline Inspection in China's thirty-one provinces all feature "Supervision and Exposure" (*jiandu baoguang*) pages, which publicize typical cases (*dianxing anli*) of disciplinary issues within their provinces to serve as warnings.[77] These typical cases include violations of the Central Eight-Point Regulations (*zhongyang baxiang guiding*), corruption cases, formalism and bureaucratism cases, and other instances of improper conduct (*buzheng zhifeng*).[78] By searching with keywords (i.e., formalism, bureaucratism), we collected 939 typical cases of bureaucratism and formalism reported by provincial Commissions for Discipline Inspection nationwide from 2020 to 2024, averaging 30.3 cases per province. For each case, we recorded the personal information of the reported official (e.g., name and position), their affiliated department (name of the functional department or type of local administrative jurisdiction), administrative rank, whether they were the primary leader of their jurisdiction, and categorized the type of reported behavior. We first conducted a preliminary screening of the report texts using keywords corresponding to the four behavioral types listed in Table 12, followed by a manual review of each case text to verify the accuracy of the initial classification and make necessary adjustments. As discussed in Section 4.2, an individual

[77] For example, the Supervision and Exposure page of the Hunan Province Commission for Discipline Inspection is available at: www.sxfj.gov.cn/jian_du_ju_bao/jian_du_bao_guang/, last accessed May 19, 2025.

[78] The majority of these reported typical cases are violations of Central Eight-Point Regulations and corruption cases, and formalism and bureaucratism only constitute a small proportion.

Table 12 Keywords for categorizing officials' behaviors

Behavior types	**Keywords**
Non-implementation	Inaction (*buzuowei*), non-completion (*wei wancheng*), inadequate implementation of duties (*luoshi lüzhi budaowei*), failure to address (*buchuli*), failure to report (*bubaogao*)
Over-implementation	One-size-fits-all (*yidaoqie*), layer-upon-layer escalation (*cengceng jiama*), excessive documentation (*guodu liuheng*), excessive accountability (*guodu wenze*), frequent repetition (*pinfan chongfu*)
Performative implementation	A mountain of documents and a sea of meetings (*wenshan huihai*), image projects (*xingxiang gongcheng*), performance projects (*zhengji gongcheng*), exaggeration (*kuada fukua*), going through the motions (*zouguochang*), perfunctory response to inspections (*yingfu jiancha*)
Selective implementation	Only did . . . did not (*zhizuo . . . weizuo*), while failed to implement (*tongshi wei luoshi*), failure to properly perform duties (*wei zhengque lvzhi*), selective enforcement (*xuanzexing zhifa*)

case may simultaneously belong to multiple behavioral types. Through classification, we found that 722 cases involved non-implementation, 94 cases involved over-implementation, 151 cases involved performative implementation, and 220 cases involved selective implementation.

We must acknowledge that these cases do not constitute a representative national sample. The description of "typical cases" on the Commission for Discipline Inspection websites indicates that they are highly selective. Every day, thousands of instances of formalism and bureaucratism may occur across various localities and departments in a province, but only a small fraction are discovered and investigated by the Commission. Among those investigated, an even smaller number are publicized as typical cases on provincial Commission websites. Additionally, the mechanisms for publicizing cases vary across provinces. Some provinces only publish typical cases investigated by the provincial Commission, while others periodically republish cases identified by lower-level (municipal or county) Commissions. These factors lead to significant variation in the number of typical cases publicized by each province. In our original dataset, the provinces with the most publicized cases were Yunnan (eighty-eight), Guizhou (eighty-two), and Zhejiang (seventy-six),

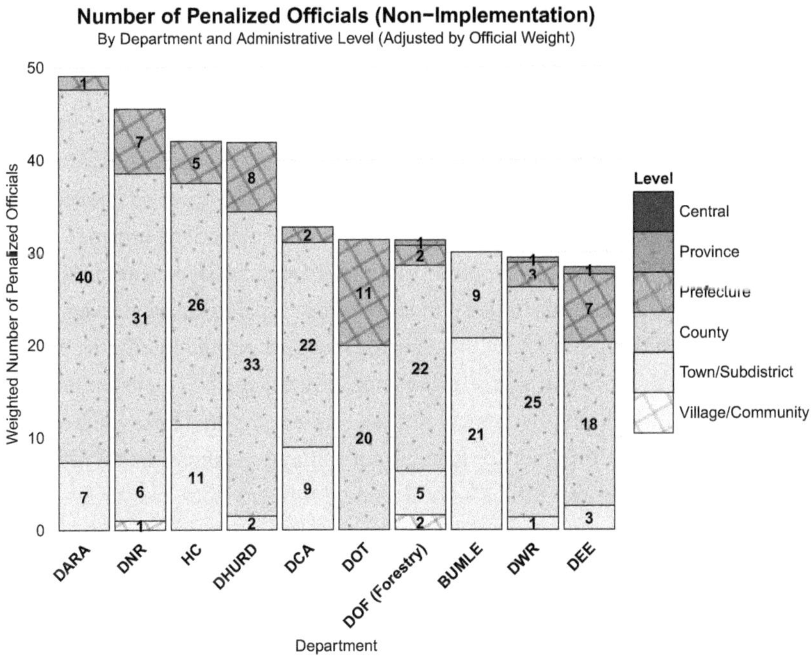

Figure 7 Typical cases of non-implementation.

Note: For the abbreviations used in the figure, please refer to Table 3 for corresponding department names. Bar heights reflect the unweighted counts, and consequently bars associated with the same integer may vary slightly in height.

while the three with the fewest were Guangxi (seven), Ningxia (seven), and Xinjiang (six). To prevent provinces with an abnormally large number of reported cases from skewing our analysis, we weighted the cases based on the permanent resident population (*changzhu renkou*) of each province in 2024.[79] After weighting, the three provinces with the highest case counts were Guangdong (eighty-five), Shandong (sixty-seven), and Henan (sixty-five), while the three with the lowest were Ningxia (five), Qinghai (four), and Tibet (two).[80] To maintain consistency with the analysis in earlier sections, we focus on the distribution of formalism and bureaucratism behaviors within government functional departments. Therefore, we excluded cases related to the heads of administrative jurisdictions (city, county, township, etc.) or party functional departments (publicity, organization, political and legal affairs, etc.). Additionally, we distinguished the administrative levels of the officials involved in the reported cases.

79 This practice assumes that formalism and bureaucratism occur in proportion to population size, with more populous areas having more cases.

80 Weighted case counts with decimals were rounded to the nearest integer.

Non-implementation is the most common category among all types of reported behaviors. Figure 7 shows the distribution of weighted non-implementation cases across different departments and levels. It can be seen that the vast majority of non-implementation cases are concentrated at the county level and below. As analyzed in Section 4.2, a key prerequisite for non-implementation is that superiors cannot clearly determine whether subordinates have genuinely achieved their intended goals, and verifying whether many policy objectives are met at the grassroots level is indeed challenging. Taking the Department of Agriculture and Rural Affairs, which has the highest number of non-implementation cases, as an example, a significant portion of the reported cases are related to officials failing to promptly address illegal use or occupation of farmland.[81] To ensure national food security, the central government has established strict red lines for farmland protection and holds officials accountable for failing to address illegal land use. However, for grassroots officials, protecting farmland does not bring direct benefits (e.g., increase in salary or promotion). On the contrary, identifying and addressing individual cases of illegal land use incurs significant administrative costs and carries certain implementation risks. Unlike more visible issues such as environmental pollution, whether farmland is illegally occupied involves more specialized information, such as land classification, which is difficult for ordinary people to assess through simple observation. When superiors cannot clearly grasp the situation at the grassroots level, local cadres thus often turn a blind eye to illegal farmland use. The situation is similar for the Department of Natural Resources, ranked second, and the Department of Housing and Urban-Rural Development, ranked fourth. The Department of Natural Resources is responsible for protecting natural resources like minerals, and many non-implementation cases involve grassroots officials failing to promptly address illegal mining.[82] Meanwhile, the Department of Housing and Urban-Rural Development is tasked with addressing illegal construction, which in rural areas often coincides with illegal farmland occupation. Due to the relative concealment of these issues and risk aversion, cadres are prone to turning a blind eye to illegal constructions.[83] The Health Commission and the Civil Affairs Department, also ranked high, are often associated with non-implementation issues related to the misuse of medical insurance and social security funds. Similar to the cases of illegal farmland

[81] See, for example, http://ynjjjc.gov.cn/html/2022/yunlingyaowen_0704/110540.html, last accessed May 21, 2025.

[82] See, for example, http://ccdijl.gov.cn/tbbg/sjwtb/202009/t20200904_7453464.html, last accessed May 22, 2025.

[83] Similar to illegal farmland occupation, issues with illegal constructions are often only discovered by superiors when reported by the public or when an incident occurs. See, for example, www.hncdi.gov.cn/web/hnlzw//article.jsp?articleId=80c4c54b-4fa1-4520-9d61-50ef83a17907&channelCode=lzw_debk_jdbg_fbzf_hn_v2, last accessed May 22, 2025.

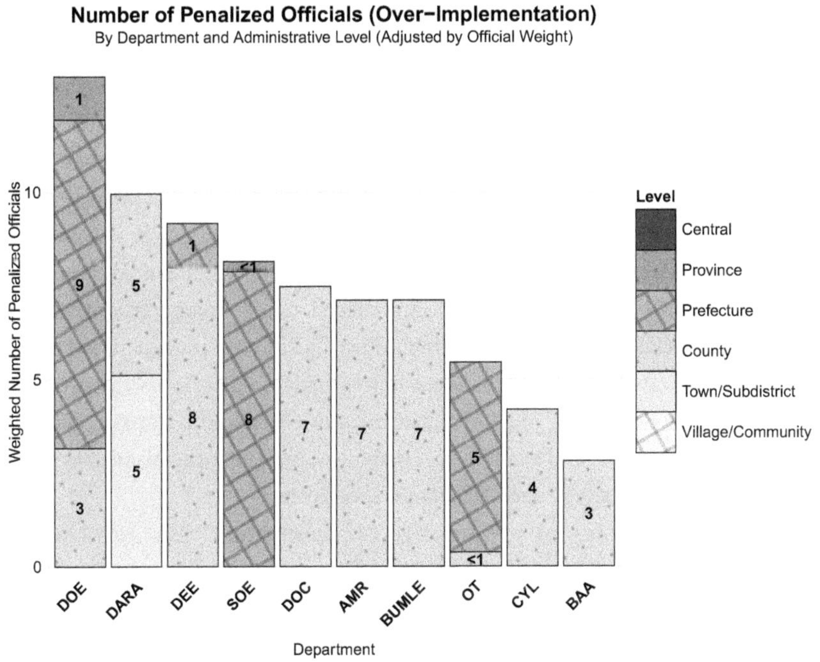

Figure 8 Typical cases of over-implementation.

Note: For the abbreviations used in the figure, please refer to Table 3 for corresponding department names. For additional abbreviations, BUMLE refers to Bureau of Urban Management and Law Enforcement, CYL refers to Communist Youth League, BAA refers to Bureau of Administrative Approval, and OT refers to others.

occupation or unauthorized construction, these behaviors are highly covert and difficult to investigate, leading to limited proactive action by officials before the issues are exposed.

Over-implementation cases are the least reported among the four types, and their numbers are even smaller when distributed across individual departments. According to Figure 8, the top three departments with the most cases are Education, Agriculture, and Rural Affairs, and Ecology and Environment. Some typical cases related to education involve campus safety.[84] Since campus and student safety issues (e.g., fires and traffic accidents) attract high social attention, any incidents can trigger public scrutiny and accountability for responsible officials. In implementing relevant policies, education departments often resort to one-size-fits-all approaches or layer-upon-layer escalation to avoid blame, such as requiring schools to conduct frequent safety inspections (to the extent of disrupting normal teaching activities) or mandating students and parents

[84] See, for example, www.ccdi.gov.cn/jdjbnew/jdjbyw/202504/t20250427_419831.html, last accessed May 22, 2025.

to repeatedly sign liability agreements. The data show that most cases related to the Education Department occur at the municipal level. Key schools (*zhongdian xuexiao*) in a city are directly managed by the municipal Education Bureau, and safety incidents in these schools tend to attract greater social attention and officials in charge thus face stronger accountability pressure, making them more prone to over-implementation. In contrast, ordinary schools (managed by district or county-level Education Bureaus) receive less attention, resulting in fewer cases. Most cases involving the Agriculture and Rural Affairs[85] and the Ecology Environment[86] departments are related to environmental protection, primarily manifested as forcibly shutting down businesses in their jurisdictions or arbitrarily fining enterprises to meet environmental targets or pass inspections. As discussed in Section 4.2, whether enterprises in a locality are causing pollution is often clearly visible, and to avoid accountability, relevant officials tend to adopt extreme measures such as one-size-fits-all shutdowns.

The highest number of performative implementation cases involves the Department of Natural Resources and the Education Department (Figure 9). Most cases in the Department of Natural Resources are concentrated at the county level and below, primarily related to image projects and face-saving projects.[87] As mentioned in this section, the main responsibility of the Department of Natural Resources is to regulate the development and use of natural resources such as land, minerals, and forests. In most cases, grassroots violations are difficult for higher authorities to detect, and local officials often turn a blind eye to such violations. However, when inspections by higher authorities take place, grassroots officials may adopt temporary measures to cover up noncompliant behaviors, such as covering roads built on illegally used farmland with soil or painting the roofs of buildings constructed on illegally occupied farmland or forests green. Inspections of natural resources like farmland by higher-level governments may not always involve on-site visits and could rely on methods like drones or satellite remote sensing, which provides further room for grassroots officials to conceal issues through face-saving projects.[88] Performative implementation cases in the Education Department are concentrated at the municipal level, primarily characterized by addressing tasks assigned

85 See, for example, www.sdjj.gov.cn/tongbao/jiandu/202312/t20231229_11690752.htm, last accessed May 22, 2025.

86 See, for example, www.nmgjjjc.gov.cn/single/2021/03/15/21031518042404829622-1805021059 1190910035.html?t=1746343548706, last accessed May 22, 2025.

87 See, for example, www.fjcdi.gov.cn/cms/html/fjsjwjw/2021-08-25/1136524971.html, last accessed May 23, 2025.

88 See, Xinhuanet.com "Painting mountains green, potted plant-style re-greening ... Exposing the chaos of disguised practices in the environmental protection field" [in Chinese] www.xinhuanet.com/politics/2019-12/23/c_1125376013.htm, last accessed May 23, 2025.

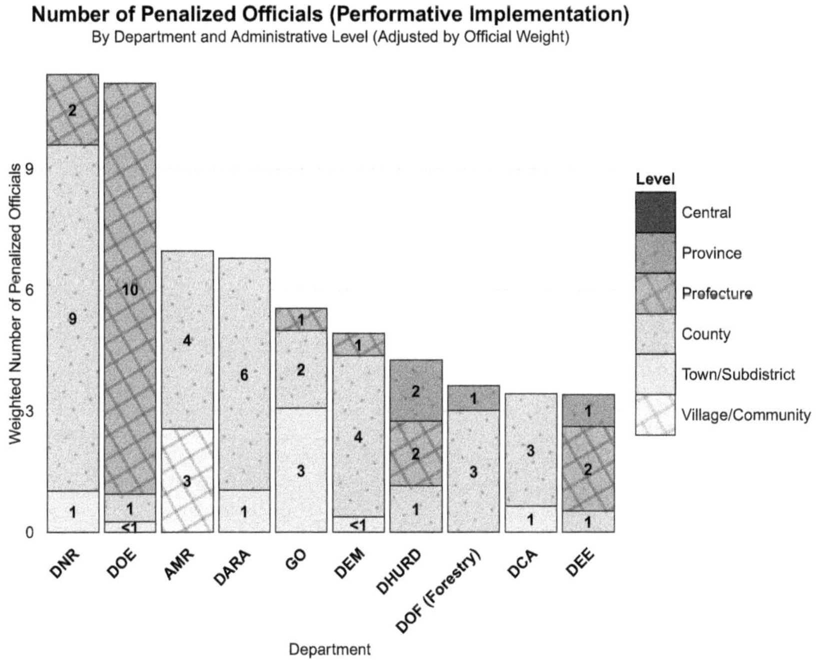

Figure 9 Typical cases of performative implementation.

Note: Since we weighted the cases based on the resident population of each province and rounded to the nearest integer, when the number of cases in a category is less than 0.5, we denote it as <1.

by superiors in a superficial, "going through the motions (*zouguochang*)" manner.[89] Compared to over-implementation cases where campus safety issues may trigger public scrutiny and lead to accountability, it is harder for superiors to observe or verify whether other tasks are genuinely implemented, such as the standardization and rectification of campus financial management. Municipal education departments often respond to superiors' requirements by forwarding documents or holding meetings, adopting a "going through the motions" approach to cope, without making substantial efforts to address the issues.

Selective implementation cases refer to situations where a case involves both active implementation or over-implementation, alongside non-implementation or performative implementation. According to Figure 10, the top three departments are Natural Resources, Housing and Urban-Rural Development, and Transportation. As mentioned earlier in this section, issues involving the Natural Resources department primarily revolve around addressing illegal land use for construction. In some

[89] See, for example, www.tjjw.gov.cn/baoguangtai/2021/06/10/detail_2021061044390.html, last accessed May 23, 2025.

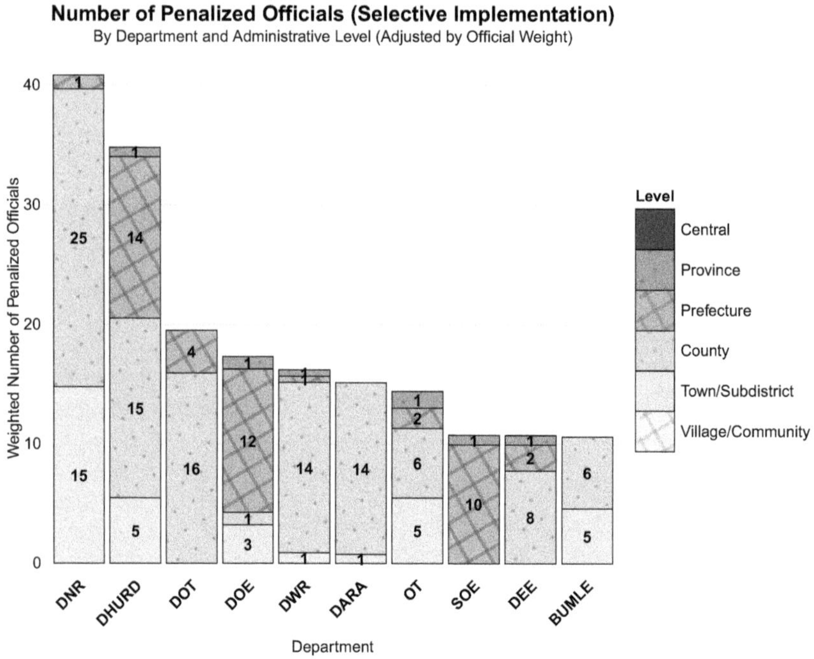

Figure 10 Typical cases of selective implementation.

Note: For the abbreviations used in the figure, please refer to Table 3 for corresponding department names. For additional abbreviations, BUMLE refers to Bureau of Urban Management and Law Enforcement, SOE refers to state-owned enterprises, and OT refers to others.

reported typical cases, grassroots Natural Resources departments officials only addressed a portion of the violations in their jurisdictions, while responding to superiors' demands for comprehensive rectification by resorting to measures such as forwarding documents or aggregating subordinate data (sometimes even falsifying data), without genuinely addressing all violation cases.[90] Similarly, the Housing and Urban-Rural Development department is responsible for addressing illegal constructions and the construction and maintenance of key public facilities (e.g., sewage and environmental facilities) within its jurisdiction. Like the Natural Resources department, some grassroots Housing and Urban-Rural Development departments only partially implement these superior requirements, while employing performative implementation or non-implementation in areas less visible to superiors to cope.[91] Selective implementation in the Transportation Bureau is primarily

[90] See, for example, http://ynjjjc.gov.cn/html/2022/tongbaopuguang_0606/109744.html, last accessed May 24, 2025.

[91] See, for example, www.zjsjw.gov.cn/quanweifabu/baoguangtai/quzhou/202010/t20201027_3013813.shtml, last accessed May 24, 2025.

concentrated on issues of arbitrary enforcement (*suiyi zhifa*) during transportation law enforcement processes.[92]

As emphasized at the beginning of this section, the typical cases published on provincial Commission for Discipline Inspection websites do not constitute a representative sample of all formalism and bureaucratism cases. However, through analyzing these different types of typical cases, their departments, and administrative levels, we can identify some common patterns. First, the majority of cases occur at the grassroots level (e.g., county level and below). In China's vast and complex bureaucratic hierarchy, the hierarchical structure itself creates barriers to information flow: Higher-level leaders cannot clearly and accurately ascertain the extent to which subordinates implement their policy intentions, and subordinate cadres have incentives to strategically gain superiors' recognition of their work or evade accountability. Under such conditions, behaviors such as performative implementation, over-implementation, non-implementation, and selective implementation become strategies for many grassroots cadres to signal active performance to superiors or mitigate implementation risks (costs).[93] Second, the top-ranked departments (e.g., Agriculture and Rural Affairs, Natural Resources, Housing and Urban-Rural Development, and Education) have core responsibilities that are difficult to measure with simple quantitative indicators. In contrast, departments like Finance and Commerce, whose work is more easily quantifiable, rarely appear among the top ranks. Moreover, the formalism and bureaucratism behaviors in these departments are often related to "risk prevention" tasks (i.e., addressing violations). As analyzed earlier in this section, tasks related to safety or risk prevention inherently pose challenges in reasonably and objectively measuring performance, making them prone to distorted incentive structures. In summary, these patterns collectively indicate that, in the presence of information asymmetry, the strategic behaviors adopted by subordinates to gain superiors' approval or evade responsibility are the primary cause of bureaucratic pathologies.

5 Conclusion and Discussions

This Element reexamines China's political selection from the perspective of attention. I argue that in a country like China, with its vast, multilayered bureaucratic system, there exists a significant issue of information asymmetry, where the capabilities and performance of subordinate officials are not self-evident. The "promotion tournament" advocated by political meritocracy relies

[92] See, for example, www.hljjjc.gov.cn/Hljjjc/html/draftNews_detail.html?publish_id=9f77f-b7211404e5a9c6f637f011606af&, last accessed, May 24, 2025.

[93] Of course, the prevalence of lower-level cases in reports may also be due to the lower political cost of disciplining lower-ranking cadres.

on the critical assumption that officials' governance performance can be measured, attributed, and compared. For functional departments, which are crucial components of the government, these assumptions are rarely fully met, yet the officials managing these departments must still compete with peers for promotions. This Element proposes that these officials' promotions are influenced by their ability to effectively capture the attention of superiors. Due to the limited nature of human attention, departments that successfully gain superiors' attention tend to have an advantage in resource allocation and career advancement. Whether a department can effectively capture superior attention is related to both the characteristics of department's functions, as well as officials' proactive efforts to seek attention and external contingencies such as sudden events. Not all efforts by officials to gain attention translate into governance performance. Many instances of formalism and bureaucratism observed in daily life are, at their core, related to officials at various levels strategically attempting to gain superior approval or evade risks and responsibilities in an environment where their real performance is difficult to assess.

The findings of this Element seek to make the following theoretical contributions. First, this study attempts to understand China's political selection through the classic information perspective in organizational studies (e.g., March & Simon, 1958; Galbraith, 1973). An official's personal traits and governance performance are not self-evident facts but rather qualities that need to be discovered, measured, and can be packaged or interpreted. Two officials with identical performance may still leave very different impressions on superiors who determine their career advancement due to varying subjective and objective conditions. In a country like China, with its vast scale, multiple hierarchical levels, and complex governance tasks, the issue of limited superior attention becomes particularly pronounced. This study provides systematic evidence on the factors that may influence an official's ability to gain the attention of superiors. Second, existing research on official selection primarily focuses on the governance outputs of territorial leaders (e.g., GDP and fiscal revenue growth). By introducing the perspective of attention, this study not only expands the scope of political selection research from territorial leaders to heads of government functional departments but also integrates the perspectives of governance outputs and officials' inputs. Whether an official can effectively capture superior attention depends not only on their governance performance but also, in areas where performance is hard to measure, on their visible work inputs (e.g., the incentives reflected in the "performative implementation" discussed in Section 4.2). Furthermore, the attention perspective also provides an integrative framework for the long-standing debate in Chinese elite selection between competence and connections. Whether through consistent excellence in their roles (demonstrating competence) or maintaining close personal ties with superiors, officials gain channels to capture superior attention, thus increasing their chances of promotion. This also explains why some studies find complementarity between competence and connections (e.g., Jia, Kudamatsu, & Seim, 2015). Finally, the attention-based perspective helps explain why China's national governance achieves remarkable success in some areas (e.g., economic growth and infrastructure development) while encountering significant issues in others (Zhou, 2014). China's top-down official management system incentivizes officials to invest more effort in areas where performance is easily observable, while in other areas, they are more likely to adopt perfunctory or distorted implementation strategies to cope.

Although the empirical analysis in this Element focuses only on specific levels and government functional departments, its conclusions have broader explanatory power. Existing studies suggest that the party has different expectations for cadres at different levels: For grassroots cadres, the emphasis is on their demonstrated governance performance, while for higher-level cadres closer to the central leadership, political loyalty is prioritized (Shih, Adolph, & Liu, 2012; Landry, Lü, & Duan, 2018). This implies that the strategies for capturing superior attention may vary across different levels. For grassroots cadres, they might adopt strategies such as creating exemplary cases or leveraging media publicity to showcase their capabilities, distinguishing themselves among the numerous grassroots officials. For senior cadres, whose capabilities are already proven, excessive media or public attention might risk being perceived as having political ambition (Lu & Ma, 2020). For these cadres, quietly building personal relationships with central leaders or creating opportunities for central leaders to visit their jurisdictions may be more effective and a safer strategy. Although the empirical section of this Element analyzes only government functional departments, its conclusions also apply to other institutions, such as party departments (e.g., organization, propaganda, and political and legal affairs), state-owned enterprises, and public institutions. On the one hand, the leaders of these institutions are also appointed and managed by the Party; on the other hand, compared to government departments, the performance of these institutions may be even harder to measure and compare, necessitating alternative means to gain superiors' recognition. In summary, for cadres at any level or in any type of department, effectively addressing the priorities of superior leaders and ensuring they are aware of these efforts (with specific strategies varying by level and department type) is the key to success in such a top-down system.

The attention-based perspective not only explains contemporary Chinese realities but also helps us understand Chinese history. During the imperial period, China already developed a vast bureaucratic system, which gave rise to inherent information problems (e.g., Kuhn, 1992). How officials could capture the attention of the emperor, who sat at the apex of this expansive bureaucratic system, had a significant impact on their career advancement. For example, in the eighth century, during the Tang Dynasty, an inner court emerged around the emperor. In contrast to the outer court, which consisted of formal civil and military officials, the inner court was primarily composed of Hanlin secretaries (*Hanlin xueshi*) and eunuchs. These inner court officials were part of the emperor's personal establishment, always at his disposal, assisting with tasks including drafting edicts (Dalby, 1979, pp. 586–589). Due to their constant proximity to the emperor, inner court members developed close personal relationships with him. Although their social prestige was lower than that of the formal bureaucrats in the outer court, many still achieved rapid promotions, with some Hanlin secretaries even rising to the position of chief minister (Wang & Yang, 2025, p. 41).

The findings of this Element also help us predict whether China can address certain governance challenges in the future. In 2022, China's population declined for the first time since the 1960s, and this decline has continued in subsequent years.[94] A key factor contributing to this population decline is the persistently low fertility rate. While the Chinese government successfully controlled population growth through the family planning campaign in the last century, the same bureaucratic system may struggle to promote population growth. Family planning reduced births by prohibiting unplanned pregnancies, with policy implementation outcomes that were highly measurable (the number of unplanned births) and attributable (to the jurisdictions of individuals with unauthorized pregnancies) (O'Brien & Li, 1999). Although the outcomes of policies promoting fertility are similarly measurable, attribution is much more difficult. Factors influencing people's willingness to have children are multifaceted, ranging from macroeconomic conditions to the costs of education, housing, and healthcare. This allows each department (or region) to evade responsibility, making it challenging to create strong incentives for implementation. Moreover, unlike the immediate feedback of family planning policy enforcement, the feedback cycle for fertility promotion policies is often very long (even exceeding the tenure of most officials). As analyzed in Section 4,

[94] See, Aljazeera.com, "China's population falls for third year in a row as birthrate declines." www.aljazeera.com/news/2025/1/17/chinas-population-falls-for-third-year-in-a-row-as-birthrate-declines, last accessed May 29, 2025.

rational officials are more likely to focus their efforts on areas where results can be seen more quickly within their tenure. We hope that the findings of this Element can stimulate future research to apply the attention framework to understand and interpret the diverse issues of Chinese politics in the past, present, and future.

References

Ang, Y. Y. (2016). *How China Escaped the Poverty Trap*. Cornell University Press.

Austen-Smith, D. (1993). Information and influence: Lobbying for agendas and votes. *American Journal of Political Science*, *37*(3), 799–833.

Baumgartner, F. R., & Jones, B. D. (1993). *Agendas and Instability in American Politics*. University of Chicago Press.

Baumgartner, F. R., Breunig, C., Green-Pedersen, C. et al (2009). Punctuated equilibrium in comparative perspective. *American Journal of Political Science*, *53*(3), 603–620.

Bell, D. A. (2015). *The China Model: Political Meritocracy and the Limits of Democracy*. Princeton University Press.

Bo, Z. (1996). Economic performance and political mobility: Chinese provincial leaders. *Journal of Contemporary China*, *5*(12), 135–154.

Broadbent, D. E. (1958). *Perception and Communication*. Pergamon Press.

Bueno de Mesquita, B., Smith, A., Siverson, R. M., & Morrow, J. D. (2005). *The Logic of Political Survival*. MIT Press.

Bulman, D. J., & Jaros, K. A. (2019). Leninism and local interests: How cities in China benefit from concurrent leadership appointments. *Studies in Comparative International Development*, *54*, 233–273.

Burns, J. P. (1989). *The Chinese Communist Party's Nomenklatura System*. M. E. Sharpe.

Cao, Z., & Wang, N. (2020). The inherent contradiction of authoritarian regime and Tiao-kuai relationship in China. [in Chinese] *Chinese Journal of Sociology*, *40*(4), 77–110.

Chan, H. S. (2004). Cadre personnel management in China: The nomenklatura system, 1990–1998. *The China Quarterly*, *179*, 703–734.

Chandler, A. D. (1962). *Strategy and Structure: Chapters in the History of the American Industrial Enterprise*. MIT Press.

Chen, J., Pan, J., & Xu, Y. (2016). Sources of authoritarian responsiveness: A field experiment in China. *American Journal of Political Science*, *60*(2), 383–400.

Chen, K., & Gu, Z. (2022). Pluralistic political achievements aompetition: A new explanation for promotion of Chinese local cadres. [in Chinese] *CASS Journal of Political Science*, (1), 117–128.

Chen, S. (2021). *Pishi: The Hidden Logic of Top Leadership Attention in China*. [in Chinese] World Scientific.

Chen, S., Christensen, T., & Ma, L. (2019). Competing for father's love? The politics of central government agency termination in China. *Governance, 32* (4), 761–777.

Chen, S., Christensen, T., & Ma, L. (2024). Written directives and ministerial tenure in China: A novel gauge for political performance. *Journal of Asian Public Policy, 18*(3), 650–669.

Citton, Y. (2017). *The Ecology of Attention*. John Wiley & Sons.

Dalby, M. T. (1979). Court politics in late T'ang times. In D. C. Twitchett (Eds.), *The Cambridge History of China, Volume 3: Sui and T'ang China, 589–906 AD, Part One*, (pp. 561–681). Cambridge University Press.

de Janvry, A., He, G., Sadoulet, E., Wang, S., & Zhang, Q. (2023). Subjective performance evaluation, influence activities, and bureaucratic work behavior: Evidence from China. *American Economic Review, 113*(3), 766–799.

Deutsch, J. A., & Deutsch, D. (1963). Attention: Some theoretical considerations. *Psychological Review, 70*(1), 80.

Ding, I. (2020). Performative governance. *World Politics, 72*(4), 525–556.

Ding, I., & Thompson-Brusstar, M. (2021). The anti-bureaucratic ghost in China's bureaucratic machine. *The China Quarterly, 248*(S1), 116–140.

Ding, I., & van der Kamp, D. (2024). How policy shapes politics: Uneven environmental policy implementation in China. *Journal of Contemporary China, 34*(155), 743–758.

Distelhorst, G., & Hou, Y. (2017). Constituency service under nondemocratic rule: Evidence from China. *The Journal of Politics, 79*(3), 1024–1040.

Duflo, E., Hanna, R., & Ryan, S. P. (2012). Incentives work: Getting teachers to come to school. *American Economic Review, 102*(4), 1241–1278.

Edin, M. (2003). State capacity and local agent control in China: CCP cadre management from a township perspective. *The China Quarterly, 173*, 35–52.

Evans, P., & Rauch, J. E. (1999). Bureaucracy and growth: A cross-national analysis of the effects of "Weberian" state structures on economic growth. *American Sociological Review, 64*(5), 748–765.

Fisman, R., Shi, J., Wang, Y., & Xu, R. (2018). Social ties and favoritism in Chinese science. *Journal of Political Economy, 126*(3), 1134–1171.

Fisman, R., Shi, J., Wang, Y., & Wu, W. (2020). Social ties and the selection of China's political elite. *American Economic Review, 110*(6), 1752–1781.

Francois, P., Trebbi, F., & Xiao, K. (2023). Factions in nondemocracies: Theory and evidence from the Chinese Communist Party. *Econometrica, 91*(2), 565–603.

Galbraith, J. (1973). *Designing Complex Organizations.* Addison-Wesley.

Gao, J. (2015). Pernicious manipulation of performance measures in China's cadre evaluation system. *The China Quarterly*, 223, 618–637.

Gao, J. (2021). Mitigating pernicious gaming in performance management in China: Dilemmas, strategies and challenges. *Public Performance & Management Review*, *44*(2), 321–351.

Goldstein, R., & You, H. Y. (2017). Cities as lobbyists. *American Journal of Political Science*, *61*(4), 864–876.

Gueorguiev, D. D., & Schuler, P. J. (2016). Keeping your head down: Public profiles and promotion under autocracy. *Journal of East Asian Studies*, *16*(1), 87–116.

Guo, G. (2009). China's local political budget cycles. *American Journal of Political Science*, *53*(3), 621–632.

Harding, H. (1981). *Organizing China: The Problem of Bureaucracy, 1949–1976*. Stanford University Press.

He, G., Wang, S., & Zhang, B. (2020). Watering down environmental regulation in China. *The Quarterly Journal of Economics*, *135*(4), 2135–2185.

Hicken, A. (2011). Clientelism. *Annual Review of Political Science*, *14*(1), 289–310.

Hill, R. A., & Dunbar, R. I. (2003). Social network size in humans. *Human Nature*, *14*(1), 53–72.

Holmström, B., & Milgrom, P. (1991). Multitask principal–agent analyses: Incentive contracts, asset ownership, and job design. *The Journal of Law, Economics, and Organization*, *7*(special issue), 24–52.

Huang, X., & Zhou, L. (2019). Paired competition: A new mechanism for the innovation of urban local governance. [in Chinese] *Chinese Journal of Sociology*, *39*(5), 1–38.

Jensen, M. C., & Meckling, W. H. (1976). Theory of the Firm: Managerial behavior, agency costs and ownership structure. *Journal of Financial Economics*, *3*(4), 305–360.

Ji, C., & Ma, X. (2025). Revolutionaries for railways. *Comparative Political Studies*, *58*(6), 1238–1272.

Jia, R. (2024). Pollution for promotion. *The Journal of Law, Economics, and Organization*, *41*(3), 866–892.

Jia, R., & Nie, H. (2017). Decentralization, collusion, and coal mine deaths. *Review of Economics and Statistics*, *99*(1), 105–118.

Jia, R., & Xu, Y. (2018). Rotating to the top: How career tracks matter in the Chinese Communist Party. *SSRN Working Paper*. https://papers.ssrn.com/sol3/papers.cfm?abstract_id=3613276.

Jia, R., Kudamatsu, M., & Seim, D. (2015). Political selection in China: The complementary roles of connections and performance. *Journal of the European Economic Association*, *13*(4), 631–668.

Jiang, J. (2018). Making bureaucracy work: Patronage networks, performance incentives, and economic development in China. *American Journal of Political Science*, *62*(4), 982–999.

Jiang, J., & Zeng, Y. (2020). Countering capture: Elite networks and government responsiveness in China's land market reform. *The Journal of Politics*, *82*(1), 13–28.

Jiang, J., Meng, T., & Zhang, Q. (2019). From Internet to social safety net: The policy consequences of online participation in China. *Governance*, *32*(3), 531–546.

Jiang, J., Shao, Z., & Zhang, Z. (2022). The price of probity: Anticorruption and adverse selection in the Chinese bureaucracy. *British Journal of Political Science*, *52*(1), 41–64.

Jiang, X., & Zhou, Y. (2025). When socialist legacy meets international norms: Gender quota adoption and institutional change in China. *Journal of Contemporary China*, *34*(151), 161–180.

Jones, B. D., & Baumgartner, F. R. (2005). *The Politics of Attention: How Government Prioritizes Problems*. University of Chicago Press.

Jones, B. F., & Olken, B. A. (2005). Do leaders matter? National leadership and growth since World War II. *The Quarterly Journal of Economics*, *120*(3), 835–864.

Jost, T., & Li, Y. (2025). The politics of promotion in China's foreign policy bureaucracy. *The China Quarterly*, *63*, 776–795.

Keller, F. B. (2016). Moving beyond factions: Using social network analysis to uncover patronage networks among Chinese elites. *Journal of East Asian Studies*, *16*(1), 17–41.

Kerr, S. (1975). On the folly of rewarding A, while hoping for B. *Academy of Management Journal*, *18*(4), 769–783.

Kou, C. W., & Tsai, W. H. (2014). "Sprinting with small steps" towards promotion: Solutions for the age dilemma in the CCP cadre appointment system. *The China Journal*, *71*(1), 153–171.

Kozlowski, A. C., Taddy, M., & Evans, J. A. (2019). The geometry of culture: Analyzing the meanings of class through word embeddings. *American Sociological Review*, *84*(5), 905–949.

Kuhn, P. A. (1992). *Soulstealers: The Chinese Sorcery Scare of 1768*. Harvard University Press.

Kung, J. K. S., & Chen, S. (2011). The tragedy of the nomenklatura: Career incentives and political radicalism during China's Great Leap famine. *American Political Science Review*, *105*(1), 27–45.

Landry, P. F. (2003). The political management of mayors in post-Deng China. *The Copenhagen Journal of Asian Studies*, *17*, 31–58.

Landry, P. F., Lü, X., & Duan, H. (2018). Does performance matter? Evaluating political selection along the Chinese administrative ladder. *Comparative Political Studies*, *51*(8), 1074–1105.

Lee, D. S., & Schuler, P. (2020). Testing the "China model" of meritocratic promotions: Do democracies reward less competent ministers than autocracies? *Comparative Political Studies*, *53*(3–4), 531–566.

Lei, Z., & Zhou, J. A. (2022). Private returns to public investment: Political career incentives and infrastructure investment in China. *The Journal of Politics*, *84*(1), 455–469.

Leng, N. (2025). *Politicizing Business: How Firms Are Made to Serve the Party-State in China*. Cambridge University Press.

Leng, N., & Zuo, C. (2022). Tournament style bargaining within boundaries: Setting targets in China's cadre evaluation system. *Journal of Contemporary China*, *31*(133), 116–135.

Li, H., & Zhou, L. A. (2005). Political turnover and economic performance: The incentive role of personnel control in China. *Journal of Public Economics*, *89* (9–10), 1743–1762.

Li, X., Liu, C., Weng, X., & Zhou, L. A. (2019). Target setting in tournaments: Theory and evidence from China. *The Economic Journal*, *129*(623), 2888–2915.

Li, Z., & Manion, M. (2023). The decline of factions: The impact of a broad purge on political decision making in China. *British Journal of Political Science*, *53*(3), 815–834.

Li, Z., & Yu, A. Z. (2023). The last strike: Age, career incentives and taxation in China. *Studies in Comparative International Development*, *58*(1), 55–78.

Lian, H. (2015). Competing for attention in the Chinese bureaucracy. [in Chinese] *Sociological Studies*, *31*(4), 1–26.

Liu, H. (2019). The logic of authoritarian political selection: Evidence from a conjoint experiment in China. *Political Science Research and Methods*, *7* (4), 853–870.

Liu, S. (1939). *On the Cultivation of Communist Party Members* [in Chinese] www.marxists.org/chinese/liushaoqi/1967/035.htm, last accessed May 25, 2025.

Liu, Y. (2021). The art of criminal investigation in China. *China Review*, *21*(3), 21–54.

Lorentzen, P. (2014). China's strategic censorship. *American Journal of Political Science*, *58*(2), 402–414.

Lu, F., & Ma, X. (2020). Is any publicity good publicity? Media coverage, party institutions, and authoritarian power-sharing. *Political Communication*, *36* (1), 64–82.

Lü, X., & Landry, P. F. (2014). Show me the money: Interjurisdiction political competition and fiscal extraction in China. *American Political Science Review, 108*(3), 706–722.

Ma, X. (2019). Consent to contend: The power of the masses in China's local elite bargain. *China Review, 19*(1), 1–30.

Ma, X. (2022). *Localized Bargaining: The Political Economy of China's High-Speed Railway Program*. Oxford University Press.

Ma, X., & Ma, J. (2021). Phantom of bureaucratic incentive structure: Types and causes of policy implementation distortion in grassroots governance. [in Chinese] *PKU Political Science Review, 3*, 146–164.

Ma, X., & Ma, J. (2024). Domestic policy consequences of international mega-events: Evidence from China. *World Development, 184*, 106753.

Manion, M. (1985). The cadre management system, post-Mao: The appointment, promotion, transfer and removal of party and state leaders. *The China Quarterly, 102*, 203–233.

Manion, M. (1993). *Retirement of Revolutionaries in China: Public Policies, Social Norms, Private Interests*. Princeton University Press.

Manion, M. (2023). *Political Selection in China: Rethinking Foundations and Findings*. Cambridge University Press.

Mao, Z. (1930). *Xunwu Investigation* [in Chinese]. https://marxistphilosophy.org/maozedong/mx1/031.htm, last accessed May 25, 2025.

March, J. G., & Simon, H. A. (1958). *Organizations*. John Wiley & Sons.

March, J. G., & Olson, J. P. (1983). Organizing political life: What administrative reorganization tells us about government. *American Political Science Review, 77*(2), 281–296.

Maskin, E., Qian, Y., & Xu, C. (2000). Incentives, information, and organizational form. *The Review of Economic Studies*, *67*(2), 359–378.

Meng, T., Pan, J., & Yang, P. (2017). Conditional receptivity to citizen participation: Evidence from a survey experiment in China. *Comparative Political Studies*, *50*(4), 399–433.

Mikolov, T., Yih, W. T., & Zweig, G. (2013). Linguistic regularities in continuous space word representations. In *Proceedings of the 2013 Conference of the North American Chapter of the Association for Computational Linguistics: Human Language Technologies* (pp. 746–751).

Milgrom, P., & Roberts, J. (1988). An economic approach to influence activities in organizations. *American Journal of Sociology*, 94, S154–S179.

Nathan, A. J. (1973). A factionalism model for CCP politics. *The China Quarterly*, *53*, 34–66.

Nathan, A. J. (2003). China's changing of the guard: Authoritarian resilience. *Journal of Democracy*, *14*(1), 6–17.

Nathan, A. J., & Tsai, K. S. (1995). Factionalism: A new institutionalist restatement. *The China Journal*, 34, 157–192.

Niskanen, W. A. (1971). *Bureaucracy and Representative Government*. Transaction.

O'Brien, K. J., & Li, L. (1999). Selective policy implementation in rural China. *Comparative Politics*, *31*(2), 167–186.

Ocasio, W. (1997). Towards an attention-based view of the firm. *Strategic Management Journal*, *18*(S1), 187–206.

Ocasio, W., Laamanen, T., & Vaara, E. (2018). Communication and attention dynamics: An attention-based view of strategic change. *Strategic Management Journal*, *39*(1), 155–167.

Opper, S., Nee, V., & Brehm, S. (2015). Homophily in the career mobility of China's political elite. *Social Science Research*, *54*, 332–352.

Ouchi, W. G. (1979). A conceptual framework for the design of organizational control mechanisms. *Management Science*, *25*(9), 833–848.

Pan, J. (2019). How Chinese officials use the Internet to construct their public image. *Political Science Research and Methods*, *7*(2), 197–213.

Pang, B., Keng, S., & Zhong, L. (2018). Sprinting with small steps: China's cadre management and authoritarian resilience. *The China Journal*, *80*(1), 68–93.

Payson, J. A. (2020). Cities in the statehouse: How local governments use lobbyists to secure state funding. *The Journal of Politics*, *82*(2), 403–417.

Pennington, J., Socher, R., & Manning, C. D. (2014). Glove: Global vectors for word representation. In *Proceedings of the 2014 Conference on Empirical Methods in Natural Language Processing (EMNLP)*, 1532–1543.

Perry, E. J. (2011). From mass campaigns to managed campaigns: "constructing a new socialist countryside." In S. Heilmann & E. J. Perry (Eds.), *Mao's Invisible Hand: The Political Foundations of Adaptive Governance in China*, (pp. 30–61). Cambridge University Press.

Pfeffer, J. (1981). *Power in Organizations*. Ballinger.

Pieke, F. N. (2009). *The Good Communist: Elite Training and State Building in Today's China*. Cambridge University Press.

Posner, M. I., & Boies, S. J. (1971). Components of attention. *Psychological Review*, *78*(5), 391.

Qi, B. (2016). *Qi Benyu huiyilu (Memoir of Qi Benyu)*. History of the Chinese Cultural Revolution Press.

Qian, Y., & Xu, C. (1993). Why China's economic reforms differ: The M-form hierarchy and entry/expansion of the non-state sector. *The Economics of Transition*, *1*(2), 135–170.

Robinson, J. A., & Verdier, T. (2013). The political economy of clientelism. *The Scandinavian Journal of Economics, 115*(2), 260–291.

Rodriguez, P. L., & Spirling, A. (2022). Word embeddings: What works, what doesn't, and how to tell the difference for applied research. *The Journal of Politics, 84*(1), 101–115.

Sandel, M. J. (2020). *The Tyranny of Merit: What's Become of the Common Good?* Penguin.

Scott, J. C. (1972). Patron-client politics and political change in Southeast Asia. *American Political Science Review, 66*(1), 91–113.

Shiffrin, R. M. (1988). Attention. In R. C. Atkinson, R. J. Herrnstein, G. Lindzey, & R. D. Luce (Eds.), *Stevens' Handbook of Experimental Psychology: Perception and Motivation; Learning and Cognition* (2nd ed., pp. 739–811). John Wiley & Sons.

Shih, V. C. (2008). *Factions and Finance in China: Elite Conflict and Inflation.* Cambridge University Press.

Shih, V., Adolph, C., & Liu, M. (2012). Getting ahead in the communist party: Explaining the advancement of central committee members in China. *American Political Science Review, 106*(1), 166–187.

Simon, H. A. (1971). Designing organizations for an information-rich world. In M. Greenberger (Ed.), *Computers, Communications, and the Public Interest,* (pp. 37–72). The Johns Hopkins University Press.

Stockmann, D. (2013). *Media Commercialization and Authoritarian Rule in China*. Cambridge University Press.

Styles, E. (2006). *The Psychology of Attention*. Psychology Press.

Su, F., & Tao, R. (2024). *Meritocracy or Patronage?: Political Foundations of China's Economic Transition*. Cambridge University Press.

Su, F., Tao, R., Xi, L., & Li, M. (2012). Local officials' incentives and China's economic growth: Tournament thesis reexamined and alternative explanatory framework. *China & World Economy, 20*(4), 1–18.

Treisman, A. M. (1969). Strategies and models of selective attention. *Psychological Review, 76*(3), 282.

Truex, R. (2016). *Making Autocracy Work: Representation and Responsiveness in Modern China*. Cambridge University Press.

Tsai, W. H. (2015). A unique pattern of policymaking in China's authoritarian regime: The CCP's neican/pishi model. *Asian Survey, 55*(6), 1093–1115.

Tullock, G. (1965). Entry barriers in politics. *The American Economic Review, 55*(1/2), 458–466.

Walder, A. G., Li, B., & Treiman, D. J. (2000). Politics and life chances in a state socialist regime: Dual career paths into the urban Chinese elite, 1949 to 1996. *American Sociological Review, 65*(2), 191–209.

Wallace, J. L. (2016). Juking the stats? Authoritarian information problems in China. *British Journal of Political Science*, *46*(1), 11–29.

Wang, E. H., & Yang, C. Z. (2025). *The Political Economy of China's Imperial Examination System*. Cambridge University Press.

Wang, Y., & Minzner, C. (2015). The rise of the Chinese security state. *The China Quarterly*, *222*, 339–359.

Wang, Z., Yao, Y., & Zhang, J. (2022). The competence-loyalty tradeoff in China's political selection. *Journal of Comparative Economics*, *50*(2), 369–393.

Whiting, S. H. (2001). *Power and Wealth in Rural China: The Political Economy of Institutional Change*. Cambridge University Press.

Whiting, S. H. (2004). The cadre evaluation system at the grassroots: The paradox of party rule. In B. Naughton & D. Yang (Eds.), *Holding China Together: Diversity and National Integration in the Post-Deng Era*, (pp. 101–119). Cambridge University Press.

Whyte, M. K. (1973). Bureaucracy and modernization in China: The Maoist critique. *American Sociological Review*, 38(2), 149–163.

Wiebe, M. (2024). Replicating the literature on prefecture-level meritocratic promotion in China. *Research & Politics*, *11*(1), 20531680241229875.

Williamson, O. E. (1975). *Markets and Hierarchies: Analysis and Antitrust Implications: A Study in the Economics of Internal Organization*. Free Press.

Wilson, J. Q. (1989). *Bureaucracy: What Government Agencies Do and Why They Do It*. Basic Books.

Wong, S. H. W., & Zeng, Y. (2018). Getting ahead by getting on the right track: Horizontal mobility in China's political selection process. *Journal of Contemporary China*, *27*(109), 61–84.

Wu, M., & Zhou, L. (2018). Political incentives and city construction: The visibility of public projects. [in Chinese] *Economic Research Journal*, (12), 97–111.

Xu, C. (2011). The fundamental institutions of China's reforms and development. *Journal of Economic Literature*, *49*(4), 1076–1151.

Xue, C., & Zhang, X. (2024). Promotion prospects and policy choice: Evidence from the land market in China. *Public Choice*, *200*(1), 119–147.

Yang, W. (2024). Power concentration and bottom-up information flow: Evidence from Chinese municipal congresses. *Governance*, *37*(1), 221–239.

Yao, Y., & Zhang, M. (2015). Subnational leaders and economic growth: Evidence from Chinese cities. *Journal of Economic Growth*, *20*, 405–436.

Young, M. (1958). *The Rise of the Meritocracy*. Thames and Hudson.

Zang, X. (2006). Technical training, sponsored mobility, and functional differentiation: Elite formation in China in the reform era. *Communist and Post-communist Studies*, *39*(1), 39–57.

Zhang, Y. (2014). Testing social ties against merits: The political career of provincial party chiefs in China, 1990–2007. *Journal of Chinese Political Science*, *19*, 249–265.

Zhou, E. (1963). *Opposing Bureaucratism* [in Chinese] www.marxists.org/chinese/maozedong/1968/5-050.htm, last accessed May 25, 2025.

Zhou, L. (2007). Governing China's local officials: An analysis of promotion tournament model. [in Chinese] *Economic Research Journal*, *7*, 36–50.

Zhou, L. (2014). Administrative subcontract. [in Chinese] *Chinese Journal of Sociology*, *34*(6), 1–38.

Zhou, X. (1995). Partial reform and the Chinese bureaucracy in the post-Mao era. *Comparative Political Studies*, *28*(3), 440–468.

Zhu, J. (2026). *Bribery as a Third Path to Power? Political Selection in China beyond Performance and Patronage*. Cambridge University Press.

Zuo, C. V. (2015). Promoting city leaders: The structure of political incentives in China. *The China Quarterly*, *224*, 955–984.

Acknowledgments

I have incurred substantial intellectual debts in writing this Element. I am grateful to Yuen Yuen Ang, Muyang Chen, Iza Ding, Dongya Huang, Siqin Kang, Shu Keng, Pierre Landry, Youxing Lang, Fengming Lu, Huihua Nie, Jean Oi, Long Ren, Victor Shih, Susan Shirk, Andrew Walder, Erik H. Wang, Susan Whiting, Xianglin Xu, Dali Yang, Xuedong Yang, Changdong Zhang, Shukai Zhao, Jiangnan Zhu, and to participants in seminars and conferences at the University of Chicago Center in Beijing, Chinese University of Hong Kong (Shenzhen), Fudan University, The Hang Seng University of Hong Kong, Peking University, Shanxi University Stanford Center at Peking University, Tsinghua University, and Zhejiang University for their thoughtful comments and suggestions. I also thank the series editor, Qi Zhang, for his confidence in me and in this project, and the two anonymous reviewers whose incisive feedback substantially improved the manuscript. Linduo Wang diligently made sure that I did not fall behind my writing plans. Zeyu Xu offered crucial emotional support. This Element would not have been possible without the help of my students at Peking University. Jiaqi Chen, Zhihao Chen, Changying Huang, Penglong Li, Yinzhi Lin, Jinsong Liu, Jialei Ma, Leimeng Qin, Qing Wu, Zijian Yang, and Dian Yu provided exemplary research assistance, and conversations with Jiaqi Chen, Xinyang Gao, Yinzhi Lin, Jialei Ma, Anchu Wang, Renhao Ye, Yifan Zhang, Yinsheng Zhou, and Yuan Zhou helped refine the Element's theoretical arguments and empirical analyses. I dedicate this Element to my brilliant students.

Cambridge Elements ☰

Chinese Economy and Governance

About the Series

The works in this Elements series examine China's economy, governance, and policy-making process. Members of the political and business communities will find the series a valuable guide to navigate China's complex policy and governance system and understand its business environment.

Cambridge Elements

Chinese Economy and Governance

Elements in the Series

A full series listing is available at: www.cambridge.org/ECEG

For EU product safety concerns, contact us at Calle de José Abascal, 56–1°,
28003 Madrid, Spain or eugpsr@cambridge.org.

www.ingramcontent.com/pod-product-compliance
Ingram Content Group UK Ltd.
Pitfield, Milton Keynes, MK11 3LW, UK
UKHW020842290926
15470UKWH00004B/1509
* 9 7 8 1 0 0 9 5 0 2 6 7 2 *